ESL
Active Learning Lessons

15 Complete Content-Based Units
to Reinforce Language Skills and Concepts

By Imogene Forte
& Mary Ann Pangle

Incentive Publications, Inc.
Nashville, Tennessee

Illustrated by Marta Drayton
Cover by Marta Drayton
Edited by Jennifer J. Streams

ISBN 0-86530-473-4

PRINTED IN THE UNITED STATES OF AMERICA
www.incentivepublications.com

Table of Contents

How to Use this Book

ESL Active Learning Lessons is not intended to be used as a complete curriculum and should not be perceived as such. The purpose of the lessons is to provide motivation and reinforcement for basic language skills instruction.

Each of the 15 complete content-based units may be used to reinforce language skills and concepts and to teach basic content concepts under many different circumstances and in many different ways.

Here are a few:

- As teacher-directed projects in a total class setting, with both English as a First Language and English as a Second Language students

- As introductory or motivational units or for reinforcement purposes

- In "pull-out" classrooms as one- or two-week units

- With individual students in tutorial settings (with slight adjustments made for group activities)

- With a small group of students on a skills need basis

- Selected activities may be used for homework or independent follow-up projects

- For peer tutoring, preferably pairing English-speaking students with non-English-speaking students

- Set up as learning stations for independent work with carefully developed, clearly and concisely stated directions for use

Unit Overview

Each of the fifteen units includes the following components:

Objective: Skills and concept goals for the unit are specified.

Content Focus: Each unit is built around a major content area of high interest or significant need for students of the intended age or experience level.

Materials needed: Easy-to-assemble-and-use materials necessary to carry out unit are listed.

Procedure

Introduction: Instructions are included for presenting each unit.

Vocabulary: A vocabulary list of words needed for the completion of unit activities is provided for each of the fifteen units. The lists are marked for cutting to form vocabulary word strips for practice and reinforcement. The words have been carefully selected to be of value as additions to the student's permanent speaking, listening, and reading and writing vocabularies as well as during the unit study, Therefore, it is suggested that the words be reviewed, pronounced orally, and the meaning of each word discussed before the word strips are cut apart.

Levels I, II, III, and IV activities: Each level activity includes directions for completion. In most instances, student activity pages are provided. When a level activity does not lend itself to a pencil and paper activity or follow-up, step by step instruction for its presentation are provided.

Extension Activities: Included for each activity, the extension activities will provide reinforcement for the skill or concept presented. Most extension activities constitute an additional lesson to be presented on the following day. Some provide a cooperative learning or partner activity while others may be used as individual homework or follow-up activities. All extension activities constitute a serious component of the language reinforcement process and should not be considered frivolous.

Assessment Activities: Each unit culminates with an authentic assessment activity designed to aid both students and teachers in measuring the degree of student mastery of the units' goals. A variety of high-interest product, performance and portfolio assessments are utilized to avoid boredom caused by sameness. In other words, the objective of all 15 units is twofold. While teaching and reinforcing basic language skills, the lessons are designed to help the student acquire information and understanding related to day-to-day life situations essential to the development of positive self-concept and confidence. Each unit is developed within the framework of a content base of information important to students with a limited command of the English language. Some assessment activities are accompanied by rubrics or scoring guides while others feature interactive approaches. Students will look forward to these activities, as opposed to the "Oh no, not another test" attitude that often accompanies traditional assessment methods.

Answer keys: For ease of use, answer keys are provided on page 143.

Bibliography: The annotated bibliography of other Incentive Publications books has been carefully comprised to provide additional references as needed for teachers of English as Second Language students. Information, strategies, and activities will be found to extend and enhance use of **ESL Active Learning Lessons**.

Content Focus Matrix

* Major Content Focus

✚ Activities Content Focus

Language areas are not designated since the objective of all units is to provide practice and reinforcement of basic language skills and concepts.

UNIT	Math	Social Studies	Science	Critical Thinking	Self-Awareness	Art	Health	Life Skills	Game
Detecting Directions		+		+	+	+	*	+	+
Finding Out About Fruits	+		+	+	+	+	*		+
Following Cafeteria Clues		*		+	+	+		+	+
Investigating Insects			*	+		+			+
Looking to the Future		+		+	*	+			
Managing Money	*	+		+	+	+		+	
Mastering Measurement	*			+		+			
Observing Significant Signs		*		+		+		+	+
Peering At Plants	+	+	*	+		+			
Seeking Safety First		*		+	+	+		+	+
Thinking About Animals			*	+		+			
Tracking Transportation		*		+	+	+			+
Understanding the Human Body			*		+	+	+	+	+
Using Important Information		+			+	+		*	
Watching the Weather			*	+		+	+		

Detecting Directions

Objective:

To provide practice in using the English language, developing vocabulary, applying basic language skills in everyday situations, and following directions.

Content Focus: HEALTH

Materials:

- Pencils
- Paper
- Colored pencils
- Scissors
- Die
- Markers
- Resource books
- Paper bags
- Ribbon
- Yarn

Procedure:

INTRODUCTION: Verbally introduce the Detecting Directions Unit. Take the time to physically act out each of the Detecting Directions vocabulary words. Involve students in acting out the words whenever possible. Pass out the vocabulary worksheets to be used for reference and reinforcement.

LEVEL ONE:

1. Introduce the following direction words: left, right, in, on, up, down, beside, forward, backward, under, across, out, around, ahead, behind, between, North, South, East, and West.

2. Cut out the sentence strips (page 12). Shuffle the strips.

3. Divide the class into small groups of two or four.

4. Direct the students to take turns drawing a sentence strip, reading the sentence, and following the directions.

EXTENSION:

Provide paper bags, markers, and yarn or ribbon for students to make a puppet. Let students use the puppets to practice giving and receiving directions.

EXAMPLE: *Take four steps to the left.* OR *Which is your right hand?*

LEVEL TWO:

1. Reproduce and distribute the game board sheet (page 13).

2. Provide the following directions:

   1. This game is for two players.
   2. Use cubes or beans for markers.
   3. The first player rolls a die and moves the correct number of spaces.
   4. He/she must tell what direction the picture is illustrating and say a sentence using that direction word.
      EXAMPLE: *The book is on the table.*
   5. The game continues until one player reaches "Finish."

EXTENSION:
Provide sheets of computer paper. Ask the students to trace the game board but do not trace the pictures. Then let the students draw their own pictures on the game board. Provide time for students to play the new game.

LEVEL THREE:

Lead a class discussion to review the following direction words: *left, right, in, on, up, down, east, west, north, south, beside, between, forward, backward, under, across, out, around, ahead,* and *behind.* Distribute the "Word Wizards" worksheet and provide assistance as needed for students to complete the puzzle.

EXTENSION:
Direct students to:
1. Write the direction words that are found in the "Word Wizards" activity on a piece of paper.
2. Rewrite the direction words in alphabetical order.

LEVEL FOUR:

Reproduce and distribute copies of the world map and of the accompanying worksheet (pages 15 and 16). Assist students in using the map to complete the worksheet according to the directions given.

EXTENSION:
1. Using colored pencils, color the continents on the map. Add the names of the oceans to the map and color them.
2. Play a game based on "I spy."
   EXAMPLE: *One student says, "I see Jose's country—Mexico. It is North, South, East, or West of Kim's country—Vietnam.*

ASSESSMENT: Reproduce and distribute the "Detecting Directions" performance assessment scoring key and accompanying rubric (pages 17 and 18).

Instruct students to listen carefully and respond to the directions as you read them according to the scoring key. For each direction correctly carried out, the student circles the check. For each one missed, the X is circled.

Ask each student to use the scoring key to reflect their performance, tally their score, and complete the rubric as appropriate.

ESL Active Learning Lessons
Copyright ©2001 by Incentive Publications, Inc., Nashville, TN.

Vocabulary List

Right	Forward
Left	Backward
In	Across
Out	Around
On	Ahead
Under	Behind
Up	North
Down	South
Beside	East
Between	West

Detecting Directions

LEVEL ONE: DETECTING DIRECTIONS

Raise your right hand.

Who is sitting across from you?

Put a piece of paper in the waste can.

Put your hands under the desk or table.

Stand behind your chair.

Stand between two members of your group.

Who is sitting on your left?

Walk four steps forward.

The students in the group stand in line.
Who is ahead of you? Who is behind you?

Put your left hand behind your back.

Put a pencil in your left hand.

Go out the door.

Who is sitting beside you?

Hop two steps backwards.

Put your arms around your shoulders and give yourself a hug.

What is the opposite of up? Stand up. Sit down.

ESL Active Learning Lessons
Copyright ©2001 by Incentive Publications, Inc., Nashville, TN.

Detecting Directions

Name_____ Date_____

Detecting Directions

Find the direction words in the word search below.

```
F O R W A R D B Q O N I
C Q A E L B R S Z A H R
L E F T D E A C R O S S
S A R B K T W E S M F O
F S A T G W K T I N C U
U T R G U E C H D J B T
H V O I E E A H E A D H
W E U I D N B T J W N C
J X N F I U N D E R K X
U Y D K S Y R I G H T G
P L Z B E H I N D Z L E
M H O M B Y D O A U N D
W E S T N P I R L N B O
O C J Q X G O T F M V W
D R O U T P W H O K P N
```

Name_____ Date_____

ESL Active Learning Lessons
Copyright ©2001 by Incentive Publications, Inc., Nashville, TN.

Detecting Directions

Name_____ Date_____

Detecting Directions

LEVEL FOUR: DETECTING DIRECTIONS

1. Using a resource book, write the name of the continents on the map.

2. Write the name of your native country on the map.

3. Write the names of your classmates' native countries on the map.

4. Look at the map and answer these questions using the direction words: **North, South, East,** and **West**:

   Europe is _____ of Asia.

   Australia is _____ of Asia.

   North America is _____ of South America.

   Africa is _____ of South America.

   South America is _____ of Antarctica.

   Australia is _____ of South America.

   Europe is _____ of North America.

   Antarctica is _____ of Australia.

   North America is _____ of Asia.

5. Answer these questions about your classmates' native countries. Find two countries on the map and fill in the blanks using the direction words: **North, South, East,** and **West**.

The country of _____ is _____ of _____ .
      (name of country)   *(direction)*   *(name of country)*

The country of _____ is _____ of _____ .
      (name of country)   *(direction)*   *(name of country)*

The country of _____ is _____ of _____ .
      (name of country)   *(direction)*   *(name of country)*

The country of _____ is _____ of _____ .
      (name of country)   *(direction)*   *(name of country)*

Name_____ Date_____

Detecting Directions

STUDENT SCORING KEY

Listen carefully as your teacher reads the directions. Follow the directions as quickly as you can. Keep your score as you go.

Circle the check (√) if you **ARE** able to act out the directions.

Circle the x if you **ARE NOT** sure of the meaning of the word.

DIRECTIONS:

√	x	1.	I can raise my right hand.
√	x	2.	I can put my left hand on my head.
√	x	3.	I can place my pencil in my chair.
√	x	4.	I can take my pencil out of my chair.
√	x	5.	I can put my hand on my head.
√	x	6.	I can put my pencil under my chair.
√	x	7.	I can stand up.
√	x	8.	I can sit down.
√	x	9.	I can stand beside my chair.
√	x	10.	I can hold my pencil between my feet.
√	x	11.	I can take two steps forward.
√	x	12.	I can take three steps backward.
√	x	13.	I can fold my hand across my chest.
√	x	14.	I can turn around three times.
√	x	15.	I can look straight ahead.
√	x	16.	I can put both hands behind my back.
√	x	17.	I can point to the north.
√	x	18.	I can point to the south.
√	x	19.	I can point to the east.
√	x	20.	I can point to the west.

SCORING KEY:

1. Give yourself 1 point for each check.
2. Give no points for each X.
3. Count the number of checks circled.
4. Write your total score here. _____

Name_____ Date_____

How Well Did I Do on Detecting Directions?

Good   O.K.   Not So Good

1. I can pronounce and tell the meaning of the twenty direction vocabulary words.   Rating: _____

2. I can recognize direction words when I see them in print and can easily identify them in puzzles and games.   Rating: _____

3. I can use direction words in sentences.   Rating: _____

4. I can use direction words to read a map and locate countries and continents on a map.   Rating: _____

5. On the performance assessment exercise, my total score was ____ points. This means I was able to carry out ____ directions and still need to work on ____.   Rating: _____

Student Comments: _____

_____

_____

Signed: _____ *Date:* _____

Teacher Comments: _____

_____

_____

Signed: _____ *Date:* _____

Finding Out About Fruits

Objective:
To provide practice in using the English Language, developing vocabulary, and acquiring basic content concepts and skills related to fruits, how they grow, and their health benefits.

Content Focus: HEALTH

Materials:
- Worksheets
- Pencils
- Drawing paper
- Crayons

Procedure:
INTRODUCTION: Verbally introduce the "Finding Out About Fruits" Unit. If possible, show some real fruits or pictures of fruits. Call each one by name and lead the conversation to include appearance, taste, origin, and other facts such as health benefits, availability, and cost.

Present the twenty vocabulary words and discuss each one. Pass out vocabulary worksheets to be used for reference and reinforcement.

LEVEL ONE:

Distribute worksheets (page 22) and assist students in completing and discussing differences in understanding as demonstrated by the drawings.

EXTENSION:
Instruct students to work together in pairs to read the names of fruits in English to each other, listening carefully to each other read. Then provide time for them to draw pictures of the fruits and write as many names as they can in their native language.

LEVEL TWO:

Provide bananas for a discussion of look, feel, smell, etc.
Distribute worksheets and paper and provide assistance in the completion of the activity.

EXTENSION:
Assist students in making and playing "The Funny Fruit Game" according to the following directions:

1. On index cards, draw and color pictures of fruit. Make two picture cards for each fruit.

2. On one index card, draw a rotten apple with a worm in it.
3. Shuffle and deal the cards.
4. Take turns drawing cards, trying to get two matching cards.
5. Take turns drawing cards to make pairs until one partner is out of cards.
6. The person left with no cards wins the game, and the player left with the rotten apple loses the game.

LEVEL THREE:

Distribute worksheets (page 23) and paper for a partner activity. Provide assistance in completion of the activity.

EXTENSION:
Distribute the extension activity worksheet (page 24). In the space provided, have students draw and label pictures of fruits that grow on trees on one half. On the other half, have them draw pictures of fruits that grow on vines. As partner practice, allow students to describe how the fruits look and taste.

LEVEL FOUR:

Distribute the math worksheets and give assistance in completion of the activity.

EXTENSION:
Direct students to make up two story problems about fruit; exchange the problem with another set of partners in order to provide a set of problems for each partner group to solve and discuss.

PRODUCT ASSESSMENT: Distribute the worksheets and rubric (on page 26). Instruct the students to work on their own without assistance to complete each assessment activity.

OPTIONAL BONUS ACTIVITY: Make and serve fruit salad to the group, discussing the fruits used, the steps in the preparation, and the differences represented in origin, taste, appearance, availability, etc.

ESL Active Learning Lessons
Copyright ©2001 by Incentive Publications, Inc., Nashville, TN.

Vocabulary List

Divided	Health
Put	Juice
Group	Trees
Brings	Salad
Below	Vines
Directions	Ounces
Grow	Picture graph
Fold	Fresh
Pick	Pounds
Recipe	Canned

Finding Out About Fruits

LEVEL ONE: LEARNING ABOUT FRUITS

Foods are divided into groups.

Fruits are an important food group.

For good health you should eat fruit every day.

1. Look at the pictures below.

2. Read the name of each fruit.

3. Write the name of the fruit.

banana _____   lime _____

apple _____   pear _____

grapes _____   mango _____

orange _____   cherries _____

grapefruit _____

strawberries _____

cantaloupe _____

watermelon _____

Name_____ Date_____

ESL Active Learning Lessons
Copyright ©2001 by Incentive Publications, Inc., Nashville, TN.

Finding Out About Fruits

LEVEL THREE: DO YOU KNOW HOW BANANAS GET TO YOUR HOME?

1. Bananas grow on a tree.

2. Someone must pick the bananas off the tree.

3. The bananas are put into a box.

4. An airplane or boat brings the bananas to the United States.

5. A truck brings the bananas to a store in your town.

6. You or someone in your family goes to the store and buys bananas.

7. You bring the bananas home.

8. Then you eat one of the bananas!

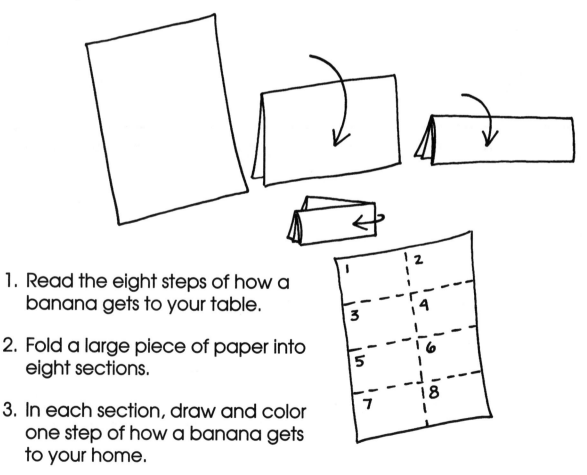

1. Read the eight steps of how a banana gets to your table.

2. Fold a large piece of paper into eight sections.

3. In each section, draw and color one step of how a banana gets to your home.

Name_____ Date_____

Finding Out About Fruits

LEVEL THREE: LEARNING ABOUT FRUITS EXTENSION ACTIVITY

Some fruits grow on trees.

Some fruits grow on vines.

Make a picture graph to show where each of these fruits grow.

Color the fruits.

Strawberries	Watermelon
Apples	Cherries
Oranges	Limes
Cantaloupe	Bananas
Grapes	Pears

FRUITS THAT GROW ON TREES.	FRUITS THAT GROW ON VINES.
_____	_____
_____	_____
_____	_____
_____	_____
_____	_____

Do more fruits grow on trees or vines? _____

Name_____ Date_____

ESL Active Learning Lessons
Copyright ©2001 by Incentive Publications, Inc., Nashville, TN.

Finding Out About Fruits

LEVEL FOUR: LEARNING ABOUT FRUITS

1. Peaches are $1.20 for three pounds.
   How much would one pound cost?

   _____

   How much would nine pounds cost?

   _____

2. One watermelon costs $2.25, and it can be cut
   into 12 pieces. There are twenty-one students in
   the class. How many watermelons are needed
   for each student to have one piece?

   _____

   How much will the watermelons cost?

   _____

   How many pieces will be left?

   _____

3. A four-pound bag of apples costs $3.60, and
   there are twelve apples in each bag.
   How much does each apple cost?

   _____

   If the bag has twenty apples, how much
   would each apple cost?

   _____

4. It takes $2\frac{1}{2}$ oranges to make one glass of juice.
   How many oranges would you need to make
   one glass of juice for each person in your family?   _____

   How many oranges would you need to make
   a glass of juice for each student in your class?

   _____

   How many oranges would you need for
   one hundred and twenty students who
   eat in the cafeteria?

   _____

5. Each student will be served three ounces of
   canned pineapple for breakfast in the school
   cafeteria. Each can of pineapple contains
   12 ounces. How many cans of pineapple
   will be needed to serve 120 students?

   _____

Name_____ Date_____

How Much Did I Find Out About Fruits?

A Lot   Some   Not Enough

1. I can identify and name at least ten fruits.   Rating: _____

2. I can tell the story of how bananas
   reach my home.   Rating: _____

3. I can name fruits that grow on trees
   and fruits that grow on vines.   Rating: _____

4. Out of five math story problems
   about fruits, I was able to solve _____. Rating: _____

Student Comments: _____

_____

_____

_____

_____

Signed: _____ *Date:* _____

Teacher Comments: _____

_____

_____

_____

_____

Signed: _____ *Date:* _____

Following Cafeteria Clues

Objective:
To provide reinforcement and practice in the use of listening, speaking, reading, and writing skills and in the acquisition of understanding and use of the school cafeteria.

Content Focus: SOCIAL STUDIES

Materials:

- Trays
- Knives
- Forks
- Spoons
- Napkins
- Papers
- Pencils
- Crayons
- Markers

Procedure:
INTRODUCTION: Discuss the school cafeteria and its use and the desirability of using good manners as both a show of respect for others and as a means of making school lunch time a pleasurable event.

LEVEL ONE:

1. Bring cafeteria items to the classroom to introduce the following vocabulary: *knife, fork, table, spoon, tray, napkin,* and *chair.* Explain and discuss the word *cashier.*

2. Distribute worksheets and instruct students to unscramble the words to match each picture.

EXTENSION:
Instruct students to draw a picture that illustrates the school cafeteria in their native country or another setting in which lunch was eaten.

LEVEL TWO:

1. Take the class to the cafeteria before a meal is served. Discuss the cafeteria procedure for getting a tray, selecting utensils, choosing food, getting napkins, paying, and finding a designated place to eat. Introduce the students to the cashier.

2. Pass out student worksheets (page 31). Instruct the students to list the items in the sequence in which they will be picked up for use in the cafeteria.

EXTENSION:
Secure from the cafeteria a tray, forks, knives, spoons, and napkins for each student. Model how to place the napkins in their laps and the correct way to hold the eating utensils. Allow time for students to practice.

LEVEL THREE:

1. Lead a class discussion about table and cafeteria manners.
2. List the manners on a chart tablet.
3. Divide the class into groups of two.
4. Play the "Please" and "Thank You" game.
5. Cut out the "Please" and "Thank You" cards.
6. Each group places the cards face down.
7. The first person draws a card. If the card reads "Please," the player asks a question or makes a statement about the cafeteria, using the word "Please." EXAMPLE: *Please give me a sandwich.*
   If the card reads "Thank You," the player makes a statement about the cafeteria, using the words "Thank You." EXAMPLE: *Thank you for the milk.*

EXTENSION:
Brainstorm with the students ways the kitchen workers help in the cafeteria. List the ideas on the chalkboard. Guide the students to write a "Thank you" letter to the cafeteria staff.

LEVEL FOUR:

Provide copies of the nutrition pyramid (page 33) and lead a class discussion of the importance of a balanced food program. Provide paper and art supplies. Ask students to work in groups to create a menu for one week that they would like the school cafeteria to use. Discuss availability of items and budgetary restrictions as preparation for the group activity.

EXTENSION
Ask students to work in groups to compare menus and discuss similarities and differences of the menus with foods they would have eaten for lunch in their native countries. Ask them to draw food items from each person's menu to make one composite balanced menu acceptable to the total group. Ask each group to draw and label the final menu to display as part of a class exhibit to stimulate further discussion.

Assessment: FOLLOWING CAFETERIA CLUES PERFORMANCE ASSESSMENT
1. Instruct students to make a Following Cafeteria Clues Booklet according to the following directions:.
2. Cut 2 pieces of white paper $8\frac{1}{2}$ x 11 inches in half, to make 4 sections.
3. Write the following topics on sections (one topic on each section):
   a. Title page
   b. Cafeteria Tray Set with Knife, Fork, Spoon, and Napkin
   c. Cafeteria Vocabulary Words
   d. Cafeteria Manners
4. Illustrate and staple the booklets together.

Review each student's completed booklet and discuss with the student his or her understanding of the function of the cafeteria and its use. Provide time for each student to check the appropriate box to denote his or her appraisal of individual achievement level in regard to "Following Cafeteria Clues."

Vocabulary List

Cafeteria	Paying
Food	Manners
Tray	Table
Plate	Menu
Fork	Lunch
Spoon	Served
Knife	Selecting
Napkin	Eat
Cashier	Please
Utensils	Thank you

Following Cafeteria Clues

LEVEL ONE _____

DIRECTIONS: Write the following mixed-up words correctly:

oonsp _____   archi _____   rokf _____

pannik _____   ayrt _____

feink _____   balte _____   rieshca _____

Name_____ Date_____

Following Cafeteria Clues

List the following items in the order in which you will pick them up before lunch in the cafeteria.

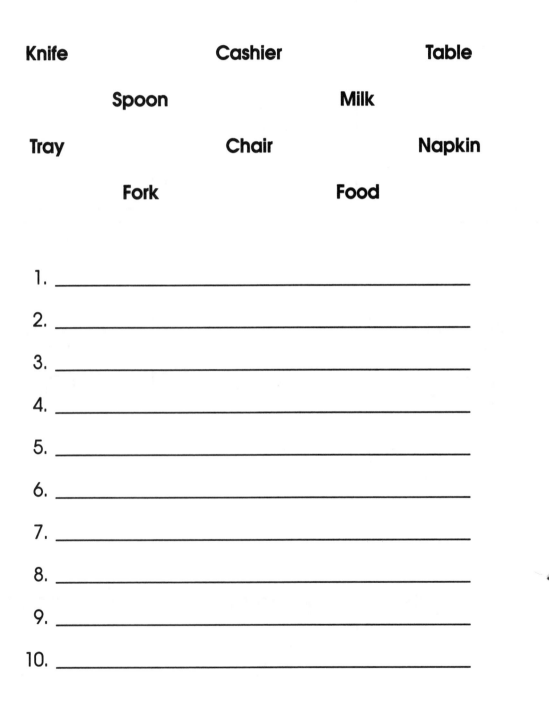

Knife   Cashier   Table

Spoon   Milk

Tray   Chair   Napkin

Fork   Food

1. _____

2. _____

3. _____

4. _____

5. _____

6. _____

7. _____

8. _____

9. _____

10. _____

Name_____ Date_____

Following Cafeteria Clues

ESL Active Learning Lessons
Copyright ©2001 by Incentive Publications, Inc., Nashville, TN.

Following Cafeteria Clues

LEVEL FOUR: NUTRITION PYRAMID

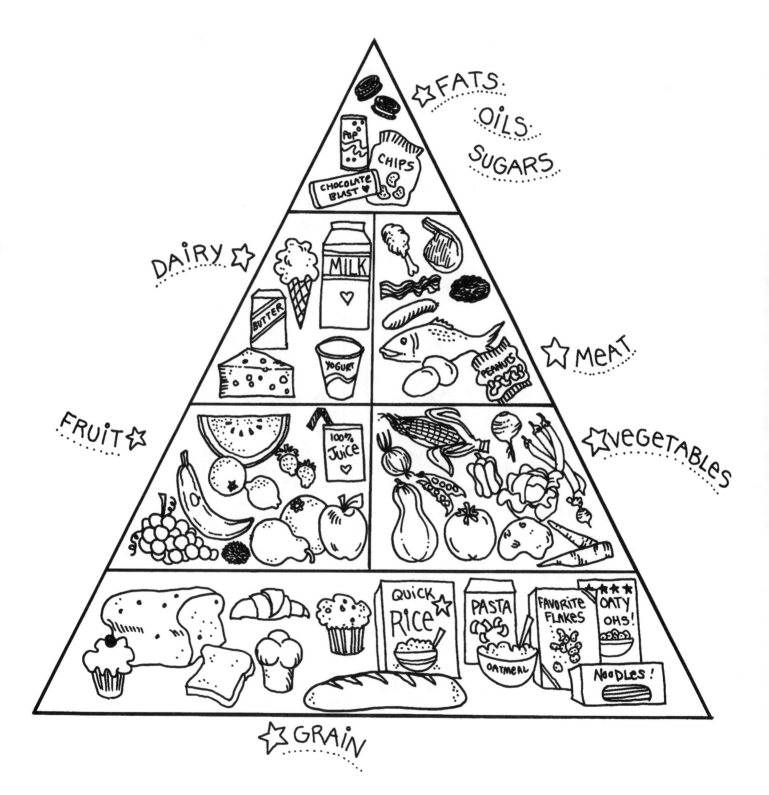

Name_____ Date_____

Following Cafeteria Clues Booklet

Check the correct box.

I think my understanding of the school cafeteria and of how to make use of it wisely and well is:

☐ very good

☐ good

☐ pretty good

☐ not good enough

Investigating Insects

Objective:

To provide reinforcement and practice in the listening, speaking, reading, and writing skills and in the acquisition of content concepts related to insects.

Content Focus: SCIENCE

Materials:
- Chart tablet
- Drawing paper
- Colored tissue paper
- Crayons
- String
- Resource books

Procedure:

INTRODUCTION: Verbally introduce the "Investigating Insects" unit. Show pictures of various insects and discuss characteristics. Present the twenty vocabulary words and discuss each one. Pass out vocabulary worksheets to be used for reference and reinforcement.

LEVEL ONE:

1. Brainstorm with the class about different insects. Write the list of insects on a chart tablet. The list might include an ant, bee, beetle, butterfly, dragonfly, flea, fly, grasshopper, mosquito, moth, termite, wasp, etc.
2. List the characteristics of insects.
3. Ask students to share information of insects in their native countries.
4. Provide resource books for students to read about insects.
5. Make a class insect identification book. Distribute worksheets (on page 38) and ask each student to research one insect and then draw and color a picture and write a paragraph about the insect. Student worksheets may then be compiled to make a class booklet for future reference.

EXTENSION:

Direct students to observe and record all of the insects that you find for one week. Use the class insect book to help identify the insects.

LEVEL TWO:

1. Print the following questions on the index cards.

   What do insects have instead of bones? ....*(hard shell)*

   How many legs do insects have? ....*(6)*

   How many main parts are in an insect's body? ...*(3 – head, abdomen, and thorax)*

   What is the life cycle of a monarch butterfly? ....*(egg, larva, pupa, adult)*

   Name two insects that live in groups. ....*(bees, wasps)*

   Is a spider an insect? Why or why not? ....*(No, it has 8 legs)*

   Name one helpful insect. Why is it helpful? ....*(bee – honey, pollinates flowers)*

   Name one harmful insect.
   Why is it harmful? ....*(mosquito: disease OR termite: damage house)*

   What do insects use to smell? ....*(antennae)*

   How do wasps protect themselves? ....*(stinging)*

2. Discuss the questions with the class. Other questions can be added.
3. Ants live in a group called a colony.
4. Travel through the ant colony on page 39 by answering an insect question.
5. Divide the class into groups of three or four.
6. At each number in the ant colony, students draw a question card, read it, and answer the question.
7. Continue until each student completes the "Ant Colony" activity.

EXTENSION:
Create an "Ant Colony" bulletin board. Provide art materials for students to create ants. Make an outline of an ant colony from brown bulletin board paper to use as a background to display the ants on the bulletin board.

LEVEL THREE:

1. Use the following points as a guide for a class discussion of the life cycle of a butterfly.
   A butterfly lays an egg.
   A caterpillar or larva comes out of the egg.
   The larva becomes a pupa where a butterfly grows.
   After 15 days, an adult butterfly emerges.
2. Provide poster board or tag board, markers, colored tissue paper, glue, scissors, and string.
3. Instruct students to create a butterfly according to the following directions:
   a. Draw a large butterfly shape.
   b. Cut out the inside of the shape, leaving a butterfly-shaped outline.
   c. Use markers to color the outline of the butterfly shape.
   d. Paste colored tissue paper over the outline of the butterfly.
   e. Attach a string and hang the butterfly from the ceiling.

EXTENSION:
Assist students in drawing the life cycle of a butterfly.

LEVEL FOUR:

1. Assist students in making a class list of insects that are harmful and helpful to human beings.
2. Ask students to draw and color insects in the "Garden Activity" (page 40).
3. Share the pictures and discuss the number of insects in each group.

EXTENSION:
Have students pretend they have brought an insect from their native country to the United States and that this insect meets an insect from America. After class discussion, direct each student to write and illustrate a story about these two insects. Provide time for sharing the stories with the total group.

ASSESSMENT: Distribute the performance assessment worksheets and rubrics (pages 41 and 42). Instruct students to work on their own without assistance to complete each of the assessment activities.

Vocabulary List

Interesting	Pupa
Insects	Adult
Characteristics	Pollinate
Observe	Flowers
Shell	Antenna
Legs	String
Head	Colony
Abdomen	Group
Thorax	Damage
Larva	Emerge

Interesting Insects

LEVEL ONE: WORKSHEET

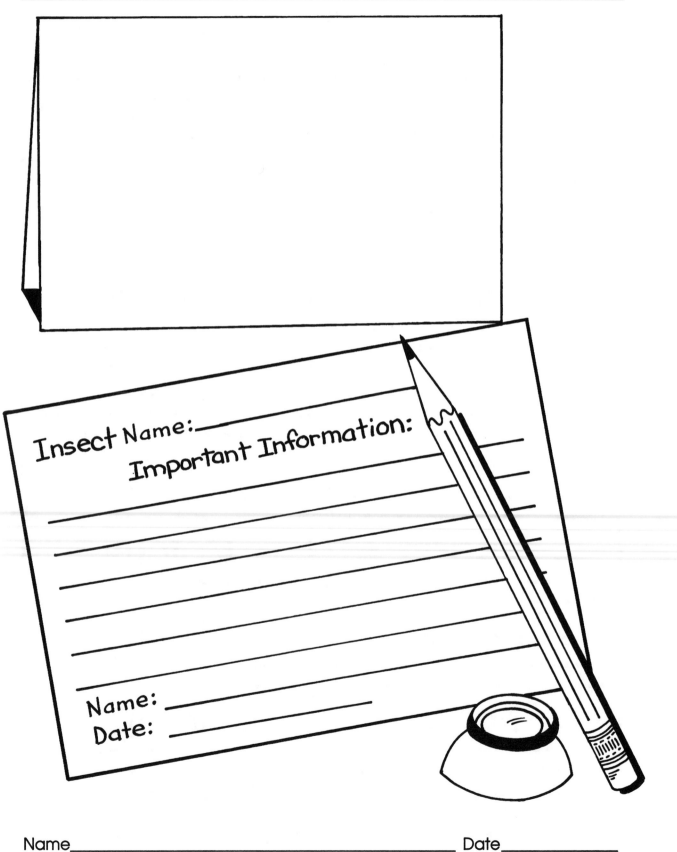

Insect Name:_____

Important Information:_____

Name: _____

Date: _____

Name_____ Date_____

Investigating Insects

LEVEL TWO: WORKSHEET

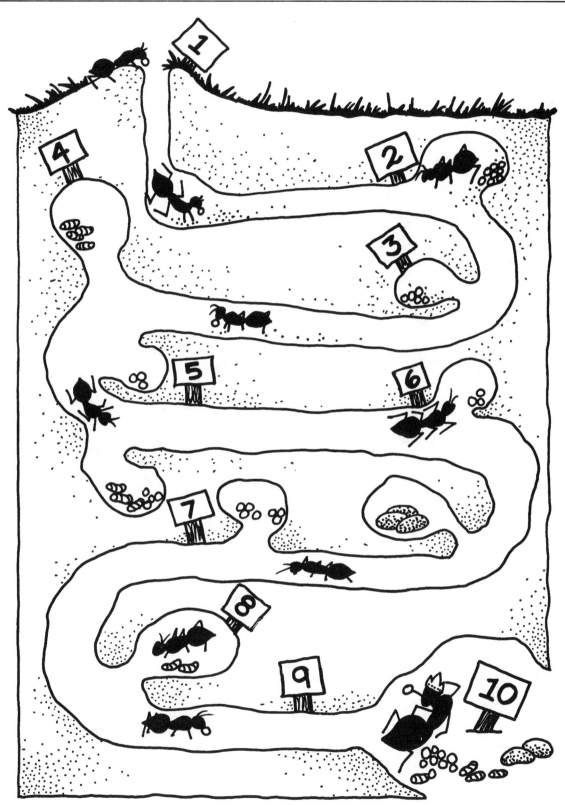

Name_____ Date_____

Investigating Insects

LEVEL FOUR: GARDEN ACTIVITY

Name_____ Date_____

Identifying Insects

PERFORMANCE ASSESSMENT

Select the correct name from the word box to identify each insect pictured.
Write the names under each picture.

Circle 😊 for each helpful insect.

Circle 🙁 for each harmful insect.

Ant	Dragonfly	Mosquito
Bee	Flea	Moth
Beetle	Fly	Termite
Butterfly	Grasshopper	Wasp

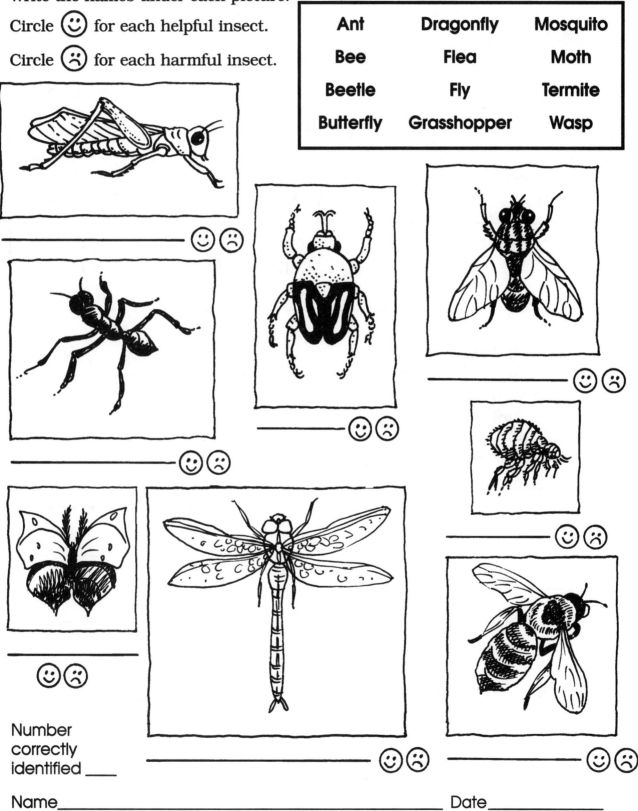

Number
correctly
identified ____

Name_____ Date_____

Investigating Insects Assessment
Rating Scale

A	**B**	**C**
Good	O.K.	Not So Good

Circle the correct letter in each box to show your Investigating Insect rating.

	A	**B**	**C**
1. Of the twenty vocabulary words, I can recognize, pronounce, and use in a sentence:	**A** 20 to 15	**B** 14 to 10	**C** fewer than 10
2. I can describe ___ insects.	**A** 15 to 10	**B** 9 to 5	**C** fewer than 5
3. I correctly identified ___.	**A** 10 or more insects	**B** 8 or more insects	**C** 7 or fewer insects
4. I can name at least five helpful insects and tell what they do.		___ Yes	___ No
5. I can tell or draw the life cycle of a butterfly.	**A**	**B**	**C**
6. Overall I think my Investigating Insects rating is:	**A**	**B**	**C**

Student Comments: _____

_____

_____

Signed: _____ *Date:* _____

Teacher Comments: _____

_____

_____

Signed: _____ *Date:* _____

ESL Active Learning Lessons
Copyright ©2001 by Incentive Publications, Inc., Nashville, TN.

Looking to the Future

Objective:

To provide reinforcement and practice in the use of listening, speaking, reading, and writing skill in the development of a positive self concept and in goal setting for the future.

Content Focus: SELF CONCEPT

Materials:
- Paper
- Markers
- Pencils
- Crayons

Procedure:

INTRODUCTION: Discuss the concept of likenesses and differences in people and the uniqueness of each individual as a "one of a kind special person." Encourage students to tell something that they feel is special about them and to identify their own physical features, country of origin, number of siblings, etc. Present the vocabulary list and go over it in a total class setting, emphasizing pronunciation and word meanings.

LEVEL ONE:

Present the worksheet on page 46 and give instructions for completing it.

EXTENSION:

Provide drawing paper and crayons and ask students to draw pictures of one thing they really like to do at school. Allow time for sharing and discussing the pictures in a total group setting.

LEVEL TWO:

Lead a class discussion to encourage students to express feelings about emotions, their causes, and their and effects. Distribute worksheets (page 47) and assist in their completion. Assist with spelling words that may not be found on the vocabulary list.

EXTENSION:

Role play various emotions, encouraging students to use body language and facial expressions to express joy, sadness, fear, anger, surprise, happiness, excitement, etc.

LEVEL THREE:

Distribute worksheets (page 48) and provide time for completing them and for a follow-up discussion. Allow students to work in groups of 3 to 4 to discuss their ideas.

EXTENSION:
Provide drawing paper and crayons or markers and ask students to draw pictures of the briefcase, toolbox, backpack, purse, or other business carry-all they would like to be carrying to work twenty years from now.

LEVEL FOUR:

Lead a class discussion of different kinds of homes, including references to homes lived in by students in their native countries. Introduce concepts related to how homes are different in different parts of the world and how homes are constantly changing because the needs and wants of the people living in them change. Present the students with pictures of a wide variety of homes if time permits. Distribute the worksheets on page 49 and provide time for completing them.

EXTENSION:
Instruct students to make lists of furnishings they would like for their "dream houses" and to illustrate the lists if time permits.

ASSESSMENT: Provide assessment rubrics (page 50) and instruct students to complete them independently.

Vocabulary List

Special	Sad
Person	Lonely
Boy	Angry
Girl	Grown-up
Years	Occupation
Old	Work
Future	Excitement
Dream	Joy
Proud	Sad
Happy	Autobiography

Looking to the Future

LEVEL ONE

An autobiography is a story that a person writes about his or her own life. The first paragraph of an autobiography should contain enough interesting facts about the person's life to make other people want to read it.

In the space below, write the first paragraph of your own autobiography. Try to include as much interesting information as you can.

My name is _____.

I was born in _____.

I am _____ years old.

One thing that makes me special is . . .

_____

_____.

Another thing is . . .

_____

_____.

Something that I am really proud of is . . .

_____

_____.

Something that I am trying to learn to do is . . .

_____

_____.

Something that I would like to do some day is . . .

_____

_____

Name_____ Date_____

Looking to the Future

LEVEL TWO

Complete the sentence beside each blank face. Draw in "faces" to show how you feel when each of the following things happen.

1. I am very happy when_____

_____

_____.

2. When I forget to do my homework I feel _____

_____

_____.

3. I feel very lonely when _____

_____

_____.

4. I feel angry when_____

_____

_____.

5. When I think of being a grown-up I feel _____

_____

_____.

Name_____ Date_____

Looking to the Future

LEVEL THREE

It is exciting to think about our future, to set goals and dream about what we want to do in the future. Put on your thinking cap and write your best answers for the following questions.

1. How old are you now? _____

2. How old will you be in twenty years? _____

3. Where would you like to be living twenty years from now?

   _____

4. What occupation would you like to be engaged in twenty years from now?

   _____

5. Circle the three reasons that most influence you to want to be in this occupation.
   a. It sounds interesting.
   b. I would be helping other people.
   c. I would make a lot of money.
   d. It would be easy work.
   e. I could have a nice home.
   f. I would work with interesting people.
   g. People would respect me.
   h. I would be able to travel.
   i. I would have a lot of free time.

Write a brief paragraph to tell what you could begin to do now to be prepared for this occupation.

_____

_____

_____

_____

Name_____ Date_____

Getting Acquainted with Myself

LEVEL FOUR

What kind of home would you like to live in twenty years from now? Would it be an apartment building, a cabin in the woods, a houseboat on the water, a two-story house, a cottage at the seashore, a mountain chalet, a condominium in the city, a farm house, or some other type of home?

Close your eyes for a few minutes and dream of the kind of home you would like to live in. Then draw a picture of your dream house below. Be sure to include the background or other features to show the setting.

Name_____ Date_____

Looking to the Future
Assessment Rubric

My Best Work

So-so

Not So Good

Draw the appropriate rating for your work in this unit next to each of the following questions.

1. I can pronounce and use the words in the vocabulary list.

2. I participated in class discussions and contributed some ideas of my own.

3. I used attentive listening skills during the class discussions.

4. My worksheets were neat and well done.

5. I worked cooperatively with my classmates when we worked in groups.

6. My autobiography was interesting and I think others would want to read it.

Student Comments: _____

_____

_____

Signed: _____ *Date:* _____

Teacher Comments: _____

_____

_____

Signed: _____ *Date:* _____

Managing Money

Objective:
To provide reinforcement and practice in the use of listening, speaking, reading, and writing skills and in the acquisition of content concepts related to money.

Content Focus: MATH

Materials:
- 10 pennies   • 5 nickels   • 19 dimes   • 4 quarters
- 2 half-dollars   • 1 1-dollar bill   • 1 5-dollar bill
  OR Paper similarities to all of the above
- Scissors   • Envelopes   • Drawing paper

Procedure:
INTRODUCTION: Display and discuss the money listed above or the paper facsimiles. Present each coin and explain its monetary value. Lead a class discussion to determine the students' understanding of money and its use.

LEVEL ONE:

Pass out the vocabulary worksheets and go over each word on the list.

Pass out the coin patterns worksheet (page 54) and instruct students to cut out the money patterns. Assist each student in arranging the pennies, nickels, dimes, quarters, and half dollars together and placing all the patterns in a row on their desks.

When the patterns are all in order, lead a class discussion to reinforce the students' understanding of the value of each denomination represented. Ask the students to hold up the correct money pattern to answer questions such as:
- How many pennies will it take to buy a candy bar that costs a dime?
- How many nickels are in a quarter?
- If you wanted to buy a book that sells for $1.00, how many quarters would you need?
- If you had a quarter and you wanted to buy a popsicle that costs $0.35, what coins could you use?

Summarize the discussion by asking students to make up questions for the rest of the class to answer. Provide envelopes for students to use to contain the coin patterns for reuse.

EXTENSION:
Provide time for students to work in pairs to make up additional questions for each other to demonstrate answers by using the money patterns.

LEVEL TWO:

Pass out the bill patterns worksheet (page 55) and instruct students to cut out the bill patterns and arrange them on their desks. Go over each bill pattern with the students before asking them to add the coin patterns from their envelopes to the display. Then ask questions such as: How many dimes does it take to equal a 1-dollar bill? How many quarters? How many half dollars? Conclude the discussion by asking more complex questions involving both coins and bills.

EXTENSION:
Following the same procedure as level one, allow time for students to work together to create questions and answers in a partner session.

LEVEL THREE:

Discuss the different kinds of stores that sell merchandise that might interest the students. Discuss stores such as as a grocery store, book store, clothing store, etc. Present the toy store worksheets on page 56 and provide time for completing them.

EXTENSION:
Provide drawing paper and crayons and instruct students to work in groups of three to draw a particular type of store containing items they would like to buy. Ask them to label each item with a price tag and make up a problem related to it. Provide time for sharing drawings and solving problems within a total group setting.

LEVEL FOUR:

Discuss the terms MAKING, SPENDING, and SAVING MONEY. Within the limits of the students' understanding, develop concepts related to budgets, saving for something one really wants, and responsible money management. Distribute the "Managing Money" worksheet (page 57) and ask students to fill in each blank with the first thought that comes into their heads, without taking time to reflect on or plan words to use.

EXTENSION:
Provide time for students to illustrate and share their completed stories with the class.

ASSESSMENT: Distribute performance assessment worksheets (pages 58 and 59) and ask students to complete them. After completion, assist in scoring the problems and discuss the various money pattern configurations that could be used to arrive at the various correct answers for the paste-up problems. Show the combinations on a chalkboard if possible. Distribute rubrics (page 60) and provide time for completion.

Vocabulary List

Money	Manage
Dollar	Hundred
Cent	Million
Penny	Coin
Nickel	Buy
Dime	Sell
Quarter	Bank
Half dollar	Price
Spend	Budget
Save	

ESL Active Learning Lessons
Copyright ©2001 by Incentive Publications, Inc., Nashville, TN.

Managing Money

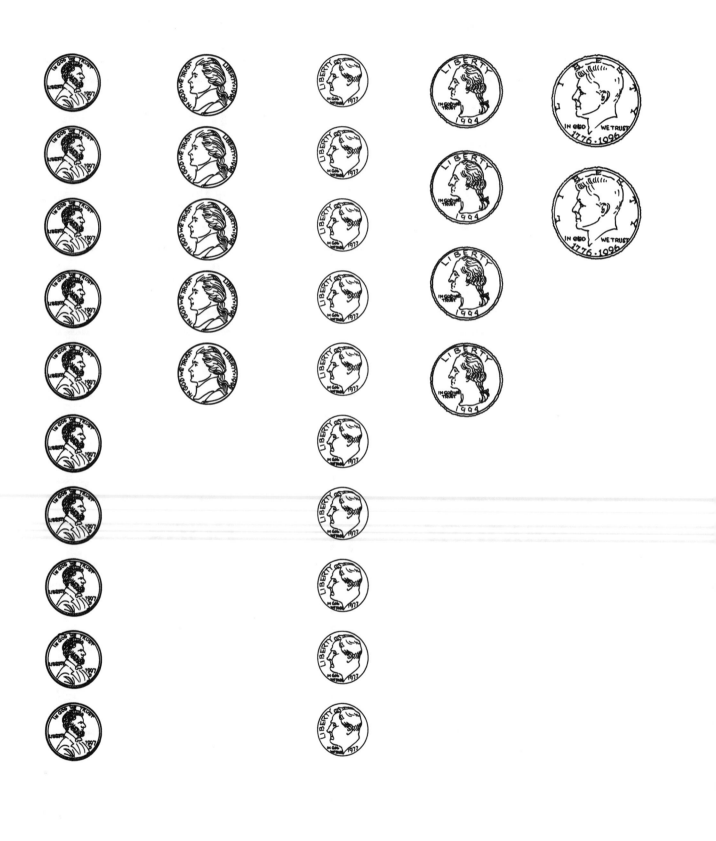

ESL Active Learning Lessons
Copyright ©2001 by Incentive Publications, Inc., Nashville, TN.

Managing Money

Managing Money

LEVEL THREE: DRAW THE MONEY YOU WOULD NEED TO BUY THE DOLL

Name_____ Date_____

Managing Money

An item I would really like to buy is a _____ .

I think this would cost about _____ .

To buy this item, I would need to go to a _____ store.

To go to this store I would have to _____

_____

_____ .

I would need to ask _____ to go with me.

I would need to take _____ dollars and the following coins:

_____

_____ .

To get this much money, I would need to _____

_____

_____ .

If I could buy this _____ , I would

_____

_____

_____ .

Name_____ Date_____

Managing Money

PERFORMANCE ASSESSMENT

Solve each of the word problems below.

Paste the money patterns from your envelope in place to show the amount of money indicated.

1. Marita has $2.00 to spend for lunch in the cafeteria. She selects a cheese sandwich that costs $0.65, an apple for $0.25, milk for $0.20, and a cupcake for $0.25. Add the price of all of the items to find out how much money she will need for lunch. _____

2. Paste money patterns here to show how much money she will need to spend for lunch.

3. Subtract the total amount of money Marita will need to spend from $2.00 to find out how much she will have left. _____

4. Paste money patterns here to show how much money Marita will have left.

5. Circle the item Marita will be able to buy for an after-school snack with the money she has left.

$ 0.40 $ 1.25 $ 0.75

Name_____ Date_____

Managing Money

6. Kim is saving her money to buy a special birthday present for her friend José. The skateboard that Kim wants to buy for José costs $7.00. Her father gave her $2.50, her grandmother sent her $3.00 in the mail, and a neighbor paid her $1.25 for pulling weeds.
   Add to find out how much money Kim has. _____

7. Paste money patterns here or on a separate page to show how much money Kim has now.

8. Subtract the total amount of money Kim has from $7.00 to find out how much more money she will need to save to buy the skateboard for José's birthday.

   _____

9. Paste money patterns here to show how much money Kim still needs to save.

10. Kim wants to buy a birthday card to go with José's present. The card she wants costs $0.95. Circle the money patterns below needed to buy the card.

Name_____ Date_____

Assessment Rubric

Make an X on your rating.

1️⃣ 2️⃣ 3️⃣	1. I can easily identify and name a penny, nickel, dime, quarter, half dollar, dollar, and five-dollar bill.
1️⃣ 2️⃣ 3️⃣	2. I can tell the value of a penny, nickel, dime, quarter, half dollar, dollar, and five-dollar bill.
1️⃣ 2️⃣ 3️⃣	3. I can count, add, and subtract money in order to solve problems involving spending and saving.
1️⃣ 2️⃣ 3️⃣	4. I understand how to use money in everyday life situations.

Student Comments: _____

_____

_____

Signed: _____ _Date:_ _____

Teacher Comments: _____

_____

_____

Signed: _____ _Date:_ _____

Mastering Measurement

Objective:
To provide practice and reinforcement in the use of listening, speaking, reading, and writing, developing vocabulary, and acquiring basic concepts and skills related to measurement.

Content Focus: MATH

Materials:
- Worksheets
- Pencils
- Ruler
- Yardstick
- Crayons
- Paper
- Food store newspaper ads

Procedure:
INTRODUCTION: Verbally introduce the "Mastering Measurement" Unit. Encourage students to discuss means of measurement in their native countries. Display a ruler showing inches and centimeters. Allow time for students to examine and practice measuring classroom objects. Pass out the vocabulary worksheets to be used for reference and reinforcement. After students have completed the worksheet for each of the four levels, collect the worksheets to be redistributed as part of the assessment process.

LEVEL ONE:

Distribute worksheets (page 64) and assist the groups in completing them.

EXTENSION:
Instruct students to look in their desks for objects to measure in inches and centimeters and to record the measurements.

LEVEL TWO:

Explain the following measurements that are used in the United States:
  12 inches = 1 foot (ft.)
    3 feet = 1 yard (yd.)
  36 inches = 1 yard
Using some of the examples on the worksheet (page 65), assist students in completing the activity. After the completion of the worksheet, discuss answers in a total class discussion.

EXTENSION:
Working in groups of two, measure a window, a door, and the width and length of the classroom.

LEVEL THREE:

Brainstorm with students about the supplies needed for a restaurant to open for business. List the ideas on the chalkboard. Using examples from the worksheet, help the students understand how to complete the activity on page 66.

EXTENSION:
Ask students to design a sign for the restaurant using their native language.

LEVEL FOUR:

Explain the liquid measurements used in the United States. Distribute worksheets (page 67) and assist students in completing the activity.

EXTENSION:
Ask students to work in groups of two to write four math problems based on a food store newspaper advertisement. The math problems may then be exchanged within groups to be solved.

BONUS ACTIVITY: Distribute the "Find the Word" activity sheet (page 68) and lead a class discussion of completed sentences.

ASSESSMENT: Distribute to students the Mastering Measurement Worksheet on page 69. Provide students with rulers, pencils, and scissors and ask them to complete the assessment activity. Arrange time for a brief student-teacher conference to discuss the ratings on the follow-up discussion sheet (page 70).

Vocabulary List

Ruler	Length
Yardstick	Width
Inch	Ounces
Inches	Pounds
Feet	Package
Foot	Serving
Yard	Weight
Centimeter	Weighs
Measure	Gallon
Measurement	Dozen

Mastering Measurement

LEVEL ONE: PERSONAL MEASUREMENTS

Use a ruler with inches and centimeters to measure the following body parts with a partner.

1. Thumb   _____ inches   _____ centimeters

2. Ring finger   _____ inches   _____ centimeters

3. Foot   _____ inches   _____ centimeters

4. Knee to ankle   _____ inches   _____ centimeters

5. Elbow to hand   _____ inches   _____ centimeters

6. Ear   _____ inches   _____ centimeters

7. Shoulder to elbow   _____ inches   _____ centimeters

8. Length of hair   _____ inches   _____ centimeters

9. Neck   _____ inches   _____ centimeters

10. Width of hand   _____ inches   _____ centimeters

11. Length of hand   _____ inches   _____ centimeters

12. Nose   _____ inches   _____ centimeters

Name_____ Date_____

ESL Active Learning Lessons
Copyright ©2001 by Incentive Publications, Inc., Nashville, TN.

Mastering Measurement

LEVEL TWO: MEASURING INCHES, FEET, AND YARDS

> 12 inches = 1 foot (ft.)
>
> 3 feet = 1 yard (yd.)
>
> 36 inches = 1 yard

Use the above measurements to fill in the blanks below.

1. 24 inches =   _____ feet

2. 2 yards =   _____ feet

3. 36 inches =   _____ yard

4. 1 foot and 6 inches =   _____ yards

5. 1 yard and 6 feet =   _____ yards

6. 18 inches =   _____ foot and _____ inches

7. 3 yards =   _____ feet

8. 48 inches =   _____ yard _____ inches

9. 27 inches =   _____ feet _____ inches

10. 5 yards =   _____ feet

11. 3 feet and 12 inches =   _____ feet

12. 20 inches =   _____ foot _____ inches

Name_____ Date_____

Mastering Measurement

LEVEL THREE: RESTAURANT MEASUREMENTS

Pretend that you have just bought a restaurant, but there are no supplies. Complete an order so you can prepare food to sell on the first day the restaurant is open.

> 1 pound = 16 ounces
>
> 1 dozen = 12
>
> buns = 8 per package

Foods Needed:

Supplies to Buy:

1. 4 ounces meat for each hamburger

   _____ pounds for 40 hamburgers

2. 1 bun for each hamburger

   _____ bun packages for 40 hamburgers

3. 6 cans of soda pop in each package

   _____ dozen cans for 72 people

4. 8 ounces potatoes for two small orders of French fries

   _____ pounds for 16 small French fries

5. 3 ounces rice for each serving

   _____ pounds of rice for 16 servings

6. 2 servings for each can of beans

   _____ dozen cans for 24 servings of beans

7. 5 ounces chicken for each serving

   _____ pounds for 80 servings of chicken

8. 2 cookies for each serving

   _____ dozen cookies for 60 servings

9. 4 ounces ice cream for each serving

   _____ ounces of ice cream for 12 servings

10. 8 ounces milk for each serving

    _____ ounces for 10 servings of milk

Name_____ Date_____

ESL Active Learning Lessons
Copyright ©2001 by Incentive Publications, Inc., Nashville, TN.

Mastering Measurement

Pretend that you are shopping at a food store. Use the following guide to compute your answers.

16 ounces = 1 pound	4 cups = 1 quart
8 ounces = 1 cup	8 cups = 1 half gallon

1. Bananas are $0.59 for one pound. How much will three pounds cost? _____ How many ounces are in three pounds of bananas? _____

2. I need to buy milk for 8 people. Each person will drink one cup. How much milk is needed? _____

3. Eggs cost $1.39 for each dozen. How much will 5 dozen cost? _____

4. Mother bought 1 gallon of juice. How many cups are in 1 gallon of juice? _____

5. Potatoes cost $0.50 for one pound. A 10-pound bag of potatoes cost $3.50. Would it be cheaper to buy 10 pounds of potatoes at $0.50 per pound or a 10 pound bag of potatoes for $3.50? _____

_____

_____

How much cheaper? _____

6. Cookies are $2.40 for one dozen. Mother says I can buy $\frac{1}{2}$ dozen. How many cookies will that be? _____ How much will the cookies cost? _____

7. There is a package of grapes that weighs 24 ounces. How many pounds and ounces is this? _____ pound(s) _____ ounces

8. A small potato chip bag holds 16 ounces of chips. 32 ounces are in a large potato chip bag. How many more ounces are in the large potato chip bag? _____ There are _____ pounds in the small bag and _____ pounds in the large bag.

Name_____ Date_____

Mastering Measurement

BONUS ACTIVITY: FIND THE WORD

Find and circle a word in the **word-find puzzle** to complete each of the sentences below. Mark off each word in the word-find box at the bottom of the page when you find it in the puzzle.

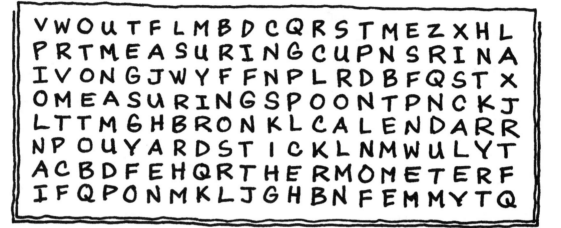

```
V W O U T F L M B D C Q R S T M E Z X H L
P R T M E A S U R I N G C U P N S R I N A
I V O N G J W Y F F N P L R D B F Q S T X
O M E A S U R I N G S P O O N T P N C K J
L T T M G H B R O N K L C A L E N D A R R
N P O U Y A R D S T I C K L N M W U L Y T
A C B D F E H Q R T H E R M O M E T E R F
I F Q P O N M K L J G H B N F E M M Y T Q
```

To measure time I would need a _____.

To measure the temperature I would need a _____.

To measure a pound of meat I would need a _____.

To measure one half yard of fabric I would need a _____.

To measure the days of the month I would need a _____.

To measure one half cup of water I would need a _____.

To measure a Tablespoon of sugar I would need a _____.

Scale	**Yardstick**	**Measuring Spoon**
Clock	**Thermometer**	**Measuring Cup**
	Calendar	

Name_____ Date_____

Mastering Measurement

MASTERING MEASUREMENT ASSESSMENT ACTIVITY

MEASURING UP

You will need a ruler, a pencil, and scissors to complete this assessment activity. Read this entire page before you begin, then go back to number one and follow the directions carefully.

1. If you correctly answered at least 10 of the 12 "Personal Measurement" problems, don't cut anything off the candy cane measurement. If you correctly answered 8 or more, cut off 1 inch. If you correctly answered fewer than 8, cut off 2 inches.

2. If you correctly answered at least 10 of the 12 "Measuring Inches, Feet and Yards" problems, don't cut anything off the candy cane. If you correctly answered 8 or more, cut off 1 inch. If you correctly answered fewer than 8, cut off 2 inches.

3. If you correctly answered at least 7 of the 10 "Restaurant Measurements" problems, don't cut anything off the candy cane measurement. If you correctly answered 5 or more, cut off 1 inch. If you correctly answered fewer than 7, cut off 2 inches.

4. If you correctly answered at least 7 of the 8 "Shopping for Groceries" problems, don't cut anything off the candy cane measurement. If you correctly answered 5 or more, cut off 1 inch. If you correctly answered fewer than 5, cut off 2 inches.

How many inches of your candy cane do you have left?

_____ inches

Circle your Mastering Measurement rating:

8 inches	6 inches	4 inches	2 inches
Super	**Good**	**Fair**	**Poor**

Name_____ Date_____

Discussion Sheet for
Mastering Measurement Assessment

1. My rating on the "mastering measurement" measuring up sheet is . . . _____.

_____

2. I think this rating is . . . _____

_____.

_____

3. I think my understanding of the use of centimeter, inches, feet, and yards is . . . _____

_____.

_____

4. I think I understand and can use the following measurements:

   a. Pound   yes   barely   no

   b. Ounces   yes   barely   no

   c. Cup   yes   barely   no

   d. Quart   yes   barely   no

   e. Half Gallon   yes   barely   no

   f. Gallon   yes   barely   no

5. I think I need more work with . . . _____

_____.

_____

6. Other things I want to discuss are . . . _____

_____

_____.

Name_____ Date_____

Observing Significant Signs

Objective:
To provide reinforcement and practice in listening, speaking, reading and writing, and in recognition of and use of important signs in everyday life.

Content Focus: SOCIAL STUDIES

Materials:
- Paper
- Pencils
- Poster board
- Markers

Procedure:
INTRODUCTION: Introduce this unit to your students and begin reviewing the vocabulary words on page 73. Discuss the signs that they are familiar with by discussing the signs that are available for viewing within your own classroom. Stress the importance of understanding signs as a helpful way of maneuvering through unfamiliar surroundings.

LEVEL ONE:

1. Lead a class discussion to identify different signs located throughout the school building that they need to be able to read (page 74). Make a list of the signs and assist the students in reading the list.
2. Take the class on a tour of the school. Provide paper and pencils for the students.
3. Ask the students to sketch the signs they see in the building.
4. Return to the classroom and share and discuss the signs observed.

EXTENSION:
1. Provide poster board and markers for students to draw and color the signs that were seen throughout the school.
2. Display the signs on the bulletin board.

LEVEL TWO:

1. Lead a class discussion related to using posters as signs. (See examples on page 75.)
2. Provide poster board and markers for students to make posters to advertise a reading contest to be sponsored by the library.
3. Display the completed posters in the school hallways.

EXTENSION:
1. Divide the class into small groups.
2. Provide a long piece of bulletin board paper and markers for each group.
3. Explain how banners are used as signs.
4. Instruct each group to create a banner for a school carnival or other celebration.

LEVEL THREE:

1. Explain to the students that businesses use signs to sell products and that these signs are called advertisements. Ask students to tell about advertisements they have seen. Write the list on the chalkboard or on a chart tablet.
2. Using the worksheet on page 76, instruct students to create advertisements that might be seen in the following places: Grocery Store, Pizza Store, Gas Station, Mall, Movie Theatre, and Pet Shop.

EXTENSION:
1. Divide the class into small groups.
2. Discuss the use of billboards.
3. Provide large pieces of bulletin board paper and markers for each group.
4. Ask each group to create a billboard.

LEVEL FOUR:

1. Lead a class discussion to create a list of different signs that the students need to know.
2. Provide time for the students to play the "Significant Sign Game" according to the following directions:
    1. This game is for two players.
    2. Each player has a marker.
    3. Place the markers on START.
    4. Write the numerals 1 and 2 on the sides of a cube.
    5. The first player throws the cube and moves the correct number of spaces.
    6. The player must say the name of the sign in the space and what the sign means.
    7. The game continues until one player reaches FINISH and wins the game.
3. Reproduce and distribute the "Significant Sign Game" worksheets.

EXTENSION:
Take a walking field trip in the neighborhood to discover all of the different signs. Provide paper and pencil for the student to list the signs that they find. Upon returning to the classroom, discuss and share the lists.

ASSESSMENT: Distribute the <u>Observing Significant Signs Performance Assessment</u> to the students.

Vocabulary List

Observing	Gym
Significant	Exit
Signs	Cafeteria
Billboard	Girls' Restroom
Advertisement	Computer Lab
Detour	Office
Enter	Auditorium
Caution	Boys' Restroom
Principal's Office	Bookstore
Library	Teachers' Workroom

Observing Significant Signs

OFFICE

Principal's Office

Boys' Restroom

Girls' Restroom

ON OFF

Cafeteria

CLOSED

Knock

GYM

OPEN

EXIT

Book Store

Stairs

COMPUTER LAB

Library

ENTER

Teachers' Workroom

Name_____ Date_____

Observing Significant Signs

Name_____ Date_____

Observing Significant Signs

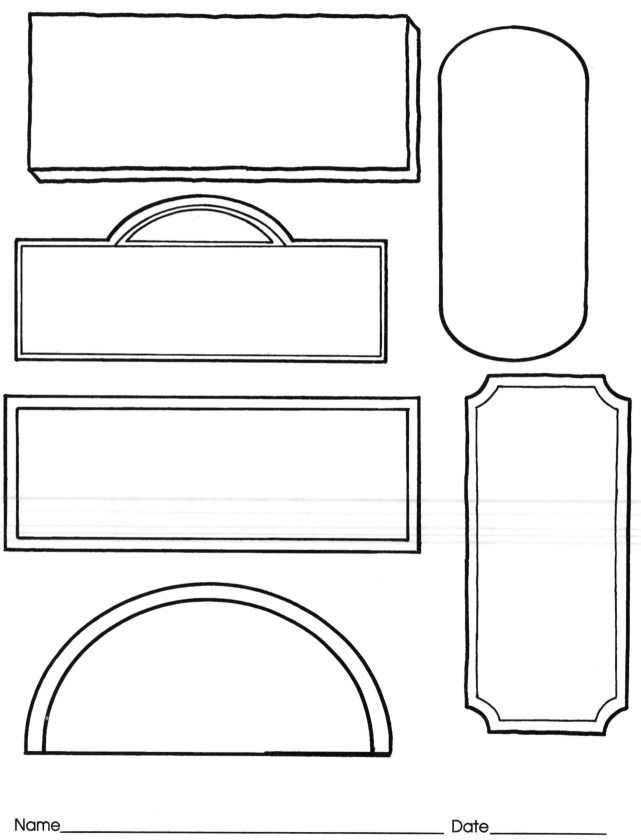

Name_____ Date_____

ESL Active Learning Lessons
Copyright ©2001 by Incentive Publications, Inc., Nashville, TN.

Observing Significant Signs

Name_____ Date_____

Observing Significant Signs

PERFORMANCE ASSESSMENT: SUMMING UP WHAT I KNOW ABOUT _____
"OBSERVING SIGNIFICANT SIGNS."

■□□ Can recognize word

■■□ Can recognize and pronounce word

■■■ Can recognize, pronounce, and tell the meaning of word

□□□ Important   □□□ Ride   □□□ Confidential

□□□ Information   □□□ Walk   □□□ Area code

□□□ Telephone   □□□ Emergency   □□□ Strangers

□□□ Phone number   □□□ Directory   □□□ Dial

□□□ Record   □□□ Long distance   □□□ Acquire

□□□ Address   □□□ Contact   □□□ Personal

    □□□ Strictly

My total score is _____.

I think this is: Good ___ Fair ___ Poor ___

Student Comments: _____

_____

_____

_____

Signed: _____ *Date:* _____

Teacher Comments: _____

_____

_____

_____

Signed: _____ *Date:* _____

Peering at Plants

Objective:
To provide reinforcement and practice in the use of listening, speaking, reading and writing skills, and the acquisition of content concepts related to plants.

Content Focus: SCIENCE

Materials:
- Drawing paper
- Measuring tape
- Pencils
- Apples
- Pint jars
- Edible seeds

Procedure:
INTRODUCTION: Verbally introduce the unit and lead a discussion of plants, asking students to draw from their own experience to contribute information about plants from their native countries. Distribute the vocabulary worksheet and discuss each word. Ask students to contribute additional words that they feel are relevant to the study of plants. List the additional words on the board and ask the contributing student to supply the word's meaning.

LEVEL ONE:

1. Lead a brainstorming session based on students' prior knowledge to create a list of plants for students to read and discuss.
2. Divide the class into small groups. Distribute worksheets and ask students to work within the group to classify the list of plants into the following categories:
   a. Plants whose fruit we can eat
   b. Plants whose seeds we eat
   c. Plants whose leaves or stems we eat
   d. Plants with no parts we eat
   e. Plants whose roots we eat

   When category lists are completed, provide time for sharing lists within a total group setting.

EXTENSION:
With students continuing to work in the same groups, provide each group with another piece of drawing paper, and ask them to cut it so that it is two feet square. Using the classified list of plants, instruct the students to draw and color each plant. Example: Plants whose fruit we eat: apple, tomato, etc. Plants whose seeds we eat: walnut, peas, etc. Plants whose leaves and or stems we eat: celery, lettuce, etc. Plants whose roots we eat: potatoes, carrots, etc. Display the pictures on the bulletin board for discussion.

LEVEL TWO:

Plan a field trip to a neighborhood grocery store after a discussion of vegetables, fruits, and grains that come from plants. After dividing the class into small groups, assign the following tasks:

1. Find and record vegetables that come from plants.
2. Find and record fruits that come from plants.
3. Find and record grains that come from plants.

Also remind the recorders to list the color of the products. If possible, take a camera to record the field trip experience. Upon returning to school, share the lists of foods.

If a field trip is not possible, substitute a classroom session using newspaper ads from grocery stores.

EXTENSION:

Provide writing paper and pencils for students to write stories about the grocery store field trip. If it is more comfortable for students to write the stories in their native language, allow them to do so. Provide time for the students to illustrate and share their completed stories.

LEVEL THREE:

1. Remind the students of procedures for using selective attention and listening strategies. Read or tell the story about Johnny Appleseed. Discuss the story and the results of Johnny Appleseed planting the apple seeds.
2. Give each student an apple that has already been cut into equal sections. Assist the students in observing, discussing, and listing the observations on a chart tablet. Ask students to find and open the seeds in the apple. After a discussion, re-read the story about Johnny Appleseed while the students eat and enjoy the apples.

EXTENSION:

Provide drawing paper and ask the students to cut it so that it will be eight inches by eight inches to form a square. Direct the students to then fold the paper in half, then fold the half into half, so that there will be four equal sections. Write the fractions for one half and one fourth on the board or a chart tablet and relate the fractions to the apple which was cut into four sections. Discuss with the students other things that can be divided into fractions. Give the students another piece of paper and direct them to experiment with the paper, dividing it into equal sections to create fractions.

LEVEL FOUR:

Lead a class discussion of the different seeds of plants that can be eaten. Fill several pint jars with different kinds of edible seeds.

EXAMPLE: *peanuts, sunflower seeds, pecans, walnuts, hickory nuts, chestnuts, etc.*

Divide the students into small groups, and ask them to estimate the number of seeds in each jar.

Then ask each group to count them to find the exact number of seeds in each jar.

Next, ask each group to work together to create posters showing various kinds of seeds, the plants they come from, how they are harvested, packaged for sale, and other features of interest related to seeds. To stimulate interest and provide examples, the *"Sunflowers From Seed to Seed"* might be reproduced, colored and mounted on construction paper and displayed as a model.

EXTENSION:
Have fun popping and eating popcorn! A lesson based on the five senses will provide an additional bonus learning experience.

ASSESSMENT: Distribute rubric and instruct students to complete it on their own.

ESL Active Learning Lessons
Copyright ©2001 by Incentive Publications, Inc., Nashville, TN.

Vocabulary List

Plants	Harvest
Bush	Sunflower
Vegetables	Stems
Grains	Roots
Grocery store	Leaves
Seed	Buds
Grow	Hulls
Popcorn	Nuts
Flowers	Sprout
Trees	Sunshine

ESL Active Learning Lessons
Copyright ©2001 by Incentive Publications, Inc., Nashville, TN.

Peering at Plants

Plants	Plants whose fruit we eat.	Plants whose seeds we eat.	Plants whose leaves or stems we eat.	Plants whose roots we eat.	Plants with no parts we eat.
White bean					
Tulip					
Cedar					
Potato					
Maple					
Grape					
Rose					
Celery					
Lettuce					
Pear					
Apple					
Carrot					
Spinach					
Pumpkin					
Persimmon					
Peanut					
Pecan					

Name_____ Date_____

Peering at Plants

LEVEL ONE

Count the number of roots, stems, leaves, fruit, and nuts we can eat. Record the number on the chart.

Roots	Stems	Leaves	Fruit	Nuts

Name_____ Date_____

Peering at Plants

LEVEL FOUR: SUNFLOWERS FROM SEED TO SEED

Peering at Plants

(Check yes or no after each question.)

1. I can explain the difference between flowers, fruit, and seeds.

   Yes __   No __

2. I can pronounce and tell the meaning of the following words:

   1. plant   Yes __   No __

   2. stem   Yes __   No __

   3. bud   Yes __   No __

   4. leaves   Yes __   No __

   5. vegetables Yes __   No __

   6. grains   Yes __   No __

   7. grow   Yes __   No __

3. I can label the parts of this plant: Yes __   No __

Student Comments: _____

_____

_____

   Signed: _____ Date: _____

Teacher Comments: _____

_____

_____

   Signed: _____ Date: _____

Seeking Safety First

Objective:
To provide reinforcement and practice in the use of listening, speaking, reading and writing and critical thinking skills and to develop awareness of the importance of knowing and observing safety precautions in every day situations.

Content Focus: SOCIAL STUDIES

Materials: • Crayons • Scissors • Masking tape • Paper plates

Procedure:
INTRODUCTION: Verbally introduce the "Seeking Safety First" unit and distribute vocabulary worksheets to be used for reference and reinforcement. Provide supplies and the following directions:

LEVEL ONE:

Distribute worksheet on page 90 to students.
1. Color the traffic light.
2. Use three paper plates to make a traffic light. Color one plate red, one plate yellow, and one plate green.
3. Use masking tape to create a street in the classroom or go outside and use a sidewalk for a street.
4. Divide the class into small groups, direct one student to portray a traffic light by holding up the colored paper plates while the other students in the group cross the street according to the light as directed by the student portraying the traffic light.

EXTENSION:
Divide the class into groups of four. Provide materials for students to draw, color, and cut out pictures of a traffic light, cars, and people. Use masking tape to create a street. Using the creative art objects, let the students pretend to drive the cars on the street or crossing the street when the traffic light shows the correct color.

LEVEL TWO:

1. Lead a class discussion related to the different kinds of transportation that students use to come to school.
   EXAMPLES: *bicycle, walking, school bus, city bus, car, van, truck, etc.*
2. List the responses of the students on the board or on a chart tablet.
3. Distribute the worksheet from page 91 and ask students to read the poem and draw a picture to show the way he or she comes to school each day.
4. Share the completed drawings and lead a class discussion of the safety rules necessary for the trip to and from school.

EXTENSION:
Select one of the creative writing sparkers below to use as the first sentence of a paragraph related to stressing the importance of "Seeking Safety First."

1. "Not obeying traffic signals can . . . "
2. "People who fail to stop for red lights . . . "
3. "Street safety rules are . . . "
4. "On my way to school today I saw . . . "

LEVEL THREE:

As preparation for introducing the "Three P's Game" lead a class discussion to brainstorm accidents that can happen in Physical Education, on a public playground, and in a park. List the ideas suggested on the board or a chart tablet.

1. Ask students to copy one of the ideas from the list on each of the squares on the "The Three P's" Game Worksheet (page 93). Additional squares can be added.
2. Cut out the squares.

Then . . .

1. Copy the second game worksheet on page 93 for each student.
2. Use the squares from brainstorming session (page 92). Ask students to draw and color pictures to illustrate each idea on the game worksheet.
3. Shuffle the "idea squares" and place them face down.
4. Taking turns, one student will draw an "idea square," read it, and say a safety rule that is important. EXAMPLE: *park, cooking hamburgers.*
   SAFETY RULE – *Be sure to put out the fire, etc.* If the student gets the safety rule correct, he/she places the "idea square" on that picture. The game continues until all of the pictures are covered.

EXTENSION:
Take the class to the playground. Ask students to demonstrate taking turns and explaining safety rules for using the playground equipment. Ask students to role play "good playground safety" and "poor playground safety."

LEVEL FOUR:

Use the story web (page 94) to write a story about safety at school. This can be an individual student story or a cooperative group activity. Add other ideas to the story web. Provide time for students to share their stories.

EXTENSION:
Provide art materials for students to create posters illustrating school safety. Invite students from another classroom to visit and view the completed art posters.

BONUS ACTIVITY: Distribute the "Danger Ahead" worksheets and provide time for completion and discussion.

ASSESSMENT: Distribute and ask students to complete the rubrics. Provide time for follow-up student-teacher conferences if possible. If time does not permit individual conferences, lead a follow-up class discussion based on student responses to the assessment worksheet.

Vocabulary List

Traffic light	Go
Street	Swings
Stop	Slide
Wait	Jungle gym
Park	Fire drill
Playground	Red
Physical education	Yellow
Safety	Green
Equipment	Cross
Game	Rules

ESL Active Learning Lessons
Copyright ©2001 by Incentive Publications, Inc., Nashville, TN.

Seeking Safety

"TRAFFIC LIGHT LINGO"

A traffic light helps people cross the street safely. A traffic light tells drivers when it is safe to go.

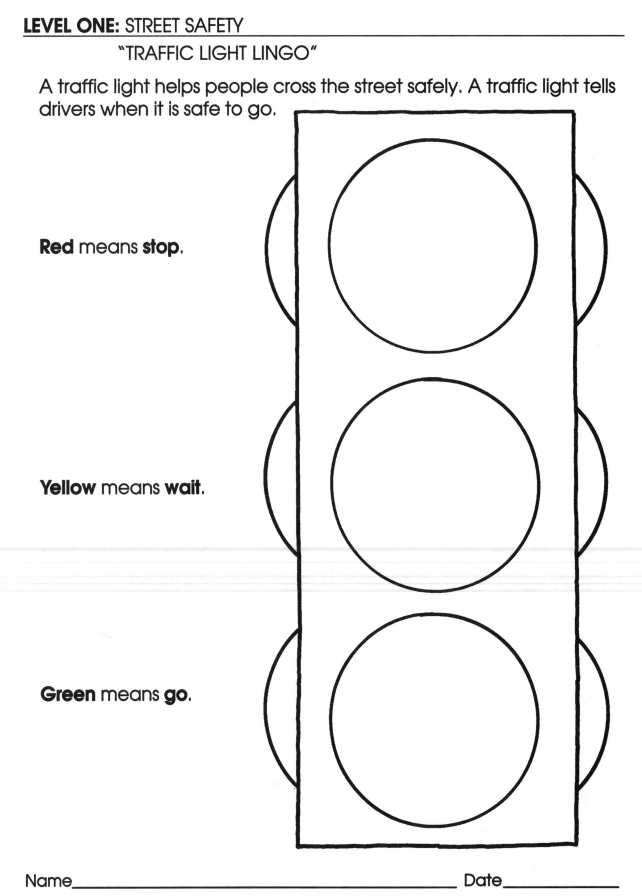

Red means **stop**.

Yellow means **wait**.

Green means **go**.

Name_____ Date_____

Seeking Safety

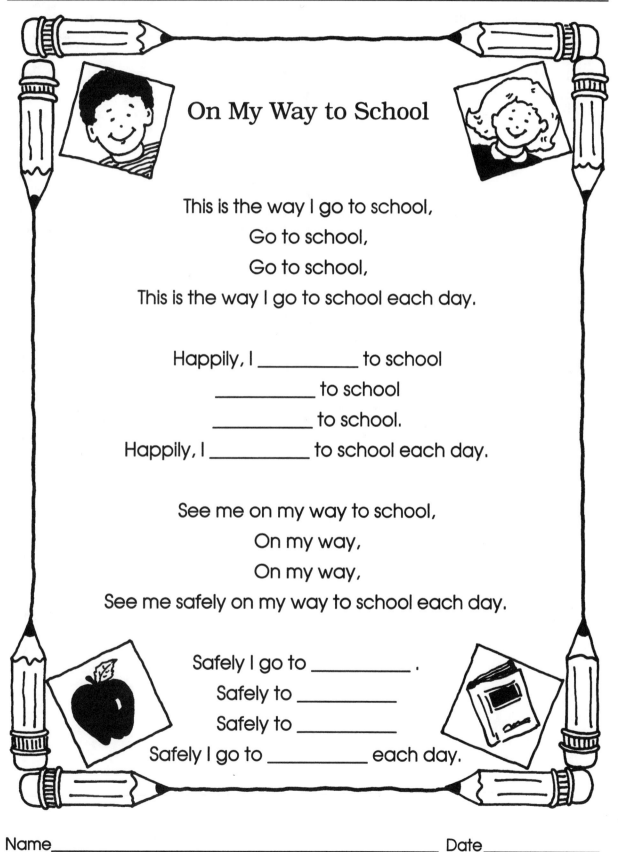

On My Way to School

This is the way I go to school,

Go to school,

Go to school,

This is the way I go to school each day.

Happily, I _____ to school

_____ to school

_____ to school.

Happily, I _____ to school each day.

See me on my way to school,

On my way,

On my way,

See me safely on my way to school each day.

Safely I go to _____ .

Safely to _____

Safely to _____

Safely I go to _____ each day.

Name_____ Date_____

Seeking Safety

LEVEL THREE: PARK, PHYSICAL EDUCATION, AND PLAYGROUND SAFETY
"THE THREE P'S"

Name_____ Date_____

ESL Active Learning Lessons
Copyright ©2001 by Incentive Publications, Inc., Nashville, TN.

Seeking Safety

Name_____ Date_____

Seeking Safety

"SCHOOL SENSE"

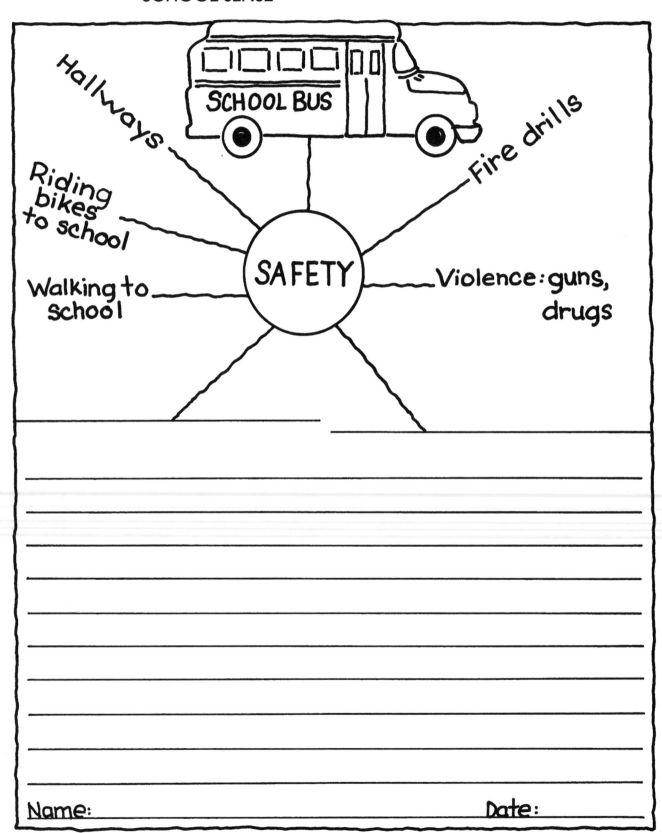

Name: _____ Date: _____

Seeking Safety

BONUS ACTIVITY: DANGER AHEAD

Find and circle 7 examples of poor safety habits in the picture below.

Name_____ Date_____

Seeking Safety First

ASSESSMENT

1. I can read, understand, and use traffic lights.	Great! Fair Needs More work
2. I can discuss street safety and follow safety rules on my way from my home to school.	Great! Fair Needs More work
3. I am aware of and able to practice good safety habits on a playground, in physical education classes, and in a public park.	Great! Fair Needs More work
4. Overall, I think my "Seeking Safety First" rating is:	Great! Fair Needs More work

Student Comments: _____

_____

_____

_____

Signed: _____ *Date:* _____

Teacher Comments: _____

_____

_____

_____

Signed: _____ *Date:* _____

Thinking About Animals

Objective:

To provide reinforcement and practice in the use of listening, speaking, reading and writing skills and the acquisition of content concepts related to animals.

Content Focus: SCIENCE

Materials:

- Pencils
- Crayons
- Scissors
- Drawing paper
- Tempera paint or colored chalk
- Newspaper
- String

Procedure:

INTRODUCTION: Lead a brainstorming session based on the students' prior knowledge to create a list of animals familiar to the students for reading and discussion. Explain to the students that some animals are born alive, while others are hatched from eggs. Tell them that animals born alive are called mammals, and that human beings are mammals. Present the vocabulary lists and discuss each word's pronunciation and meaning. Compare the vocabulary lists to the class-created list of animals.

LEVEL ONE:

1. Encourage students to tell about pets they had in their native countries. Distribute the pets vocabulary list and go over the words. Add other animals that may be mentioned by students.
2. Ask the class to describe the pet's care, food, and whether the pet lived inside or outside their houses.
3. Lead the discussion to their pets in the United States and pet stores. If possible, take a field trip to a pet store or allow students to bring a pet to school.
4. Distribute worksheet (page 101) and instruct students to label the pet in each cage in "Pietro's Pet Shop" worksheet according to the directions. Ask them to color the animal they would most like to have for a pet and tell why they like that particular animal.

EXTENSION:

Based on the "Pet Shop" activity, ask students to write or tell a story about a conversation between two pets in the Pet Shop.

LEVEL TWO:

1. Lead a brainstorming session to create a list of farm animals. Present the farm animals vocabulary list and add any words from the discussion that may not be on the list.
2. Create another list of farm animals from the students' native countries.
3. Ask students to follow the directions to complete the worksheet on page 102.

EXTENSION:

Using the list of farm animals from the worksheet, ask students to write a sentence telling how each animal is important to life on a farm.

LEVEL THREE:

1. Locate the continent of Africa on a map.
2. Provide resource books with information and pictures of African animals.
3. Explain an African Safari and present the African Animal Vocabulary list (page 100). Add to the list any additional animals mentioned by the students.
4. Ask students to pretend they are on an African Safari for the purpose of observing and taking photographs of animals that might be seen.
5. Using page 103, instruct students to draw, color, and label African animals to represent the photographs.

EXTENSION:
Instruct students to:
1. Cut out the picture "photographs."
2. Paste them on construction paper.
3. Under each picture, write two facts about the animal.

LEVEL FOUR:

1. Take the students to the library to locate resource books with sea animals as the subject. Present and discuss the sea animal vocabulary list (page 100) and add any suggestions by students.
2. In groups of two, instruct students to find and talk about different sea animals in the resource books.
3. Provide drawing paper and pencils for students to sketch and label three of their favorite sea animals. Use page 104 as a guide.
4. Upon returning to the classroom, give students two large pieces of drawing paper.
5. Ask students to draw a large outline for a fish they find interesting.
6. Next, the fish outline will be placed on another large piece of drawing paper and traced. The student now has two outlines of fish.
7. Provide tempera paint or colored chalk for the students to color and decorate the fish.
8. The two fish outlines should then be stapled together and stuffed with newspaper.
9. Finally, string should be attached to hang the fish from the ceiling.
10. Conclude the lesson by allowing students to share information about their sea animals.

EXTENSION:
Provide a copy of a world map. Ask students to label the oceans where sea animals are found. Continents can be labeled to help students understand the ocean locations.

Assessment
PERFORMANCE ASSESSMENT: Distribute worksheets (page 105) and give instructions for completion, including total number of checks for each column. Follow up by distributing rubrics (page 106) and providing time for completion.

OPTIONAL BONUS ACTIVITY: Assist students in compiling worksheets for a take-home booklet. Provide paper, art supplies, and time for making booklet covers.

Farm Animals Vocabulary List

Turkey

Chicken

Horse

Cow

Sheep

Goat

Pig

Duck

Donkey

Goose

Pets Vocabulary List

Dog

Cat

Rabbit

White mouse

Frog

Hamster

Snake

Goldfish

Parrot

Canary

Sea Animals Vocabulary List

Dolphin

Coral

Whale

Shark

Porpoise

Octopus

Tuna

Oyster

Lobster

Eel

African Animals Vocabulary List

Giraffe

Elephant

Lion

Tiger

Cheetah

Hippopotamus

Zebra

Cobra

Lizard

Leopard

Thinking About Animals

LEVEL ONE: PIETRO'S PET SHOP

Would you expect to find an elephant in a pet store? _____

Which pet would be easier to care for, a pig or a parrot? _____

Would you rather have a dog or a cat for a pet? _____

Why? _____

_____

Name_____ Date_____

Thinking About Animals

LEVEL TWO WORKSHEET: FRIENDLY FRED'S FARM

Add at least ten farm animals for this sketch of Friendly Fred's Farm.
Circle the animals that are hatched from eggs.
Make an X on the animals that are born alive.
Color the animals that have feathers.
Underline the animals that have fur.

Name_____ Date_____

ESL Active Learning Lessons
Copyright ©2001 by Incentive Publications, Inc., Nashville, TN.

Thinking About Animals

Draw and color an animal that you might see on an African Safari in each of the photo frames. Label each animal.

Name_____ Date_____

Thinking About Animals

LEVEL FOUR ACTIVITY: DIRECTIONS FOR MAKING A STUFFED FISH

Name_____ Date_____

Learning About Animals Assessment

PERFORMANCE ASSESSMENT

Complete the matrix by checking the appropriate boxes beside each animal.

Animal	Pet	Farm animal	African animal	Ocean animal	Hatched from egg	Born alive	Feathers
Elephant							
Pig							
Cow							
Dog							
Parrot							
Tiger							
Chicken							
Rabbit							
Whale							
Goldfish							
Zebra							
Horse							
Turkey							
Lion							
Tuna							
Giraffe							
Duck							
Total Number							

Name_____ Date_____

Learning about Animals

ASSESSMENT RUBRIC

| 8–10 | 5–7 | Fewer than 5 |
| Fine | O.K. | Not so Good |

Circle your rating:

I can name and identify animals that are pets.	Fine	O.K.	Not so Good
I can name and identify farm animals.	Fine	O.K.	Not so Good
I can name and identify African Animals.	Fine	O.K.	Not so Good
I can name and identify ocean animals.	Fine	O.K.	Not so Good
My drawings for the unit were original and clear.	Fine	O.K.	Not so Good
I can tell which animals are born alive and which are hatched from eggs.	Fine	O.K.	Not so Good

Student Comments: _____

_____

_____

_____

Signed: _____ *Date:* _____

Teacher Comments: _____

_____

_____

_____

Signed: _____ *Date:* _____

Tracking Transportation

Objective:
To provide practice in using the English language, developing vocabulary, and acquiring concepts and skills related to means of transportation.

Content Focus: SOCIAL STUDIES

Materials:
- Worksheets
- Pencils
- Drawing paper
- Crayons
- Scissors
- Tempera paint

Procedure:
INTRODUCTION: Verbally introduce the "Tracking Transportation" Unit. If possible, show pictures or models of model forms of transportation such as cars, trucks, buses, planes, boats, etc. Call each one by name and lead the conversation to include differences in size, construction, use, and history.

Present the twenty vocabulary words and discuss each one. Pass out vocabulary worksheets to be used for reference and reinforcement.

LEVEL ONE:

1. Discuss the vocabulary word **transportation** with the class.
2. Ask each student to make a list of different or unusual forms of transportation in his or her native country.
3. Provide time for students to share the transportation lists.
4. Give each student three pieces of drawing paper. Ask students to draw and color one example of transportation from their native country on each piece of drawing paper.
5. Mount the pictures on construction paper and display them on a bulletin board to spark conversation and interaction.

EXTENSION:
1. Give each student an $8\frac{1}{2}$ x 11-inch piece of white paper to be folded into four equal sections.
2. In each section of the paper, ask students to draw a picture of the methods of transportation that were used to transport them from their native countries to their new home in the United States.

LEVEL TWO

1. Provide art materials for students to trace and cut out one means of transportation they have used. Use page 110 as a guide.
2. Instruct students to write a sentence or a paragraph about how that mode of transportation is used since living in their new homeland.

EXTENSION:
Provide magazines for students to cut out pictures of different types of transportation to use to create collages. Provide time for discussion of each type of transportation depicted by the collage.

LEVEL THREE

1. Distribute worksheets (page 111) and instruct students to color the picture and cut on the dotted lines around the pictures to make the picture cards for the activity.
2. Divide the class into small groups.
3. Continue the activity according to the following procedure:
    a. The picture cards are placed face down for each student.
    b. The first student draws a picture card and gives clues about the picture that describes what kind of transportation it is.
       EXAMPLE: Picture card has a bicycle on it. Student might give clues: *Boys and girls ride this for fun, it has two wheels, etc.*
       EXAMPLE: Picture card has a school bus on it. Student might say: *Boys and girls ride on this to school.*
    c. The activity concludes when all the cards are used.

EXTENSION:
Using the picture cards for the "Transportation Thinking" game, write the word for each picture on an index card. Ask students to match the picture cards with the correct transportation words.

LEVEL FOUR

Play the "Transportation Trivia" game according to the following rules:
This game is for two players.

1. Cut out the transportation clue cards on page 112. Shuffle the cards and place them face down. Each answer to the clue cards is one means of transportation.
   EXAMPLE: *How would you go to school? Walk.*
2. Distribute a copy of the board game (page 113) to each pair of students.
3. Each player places a marker on "Start."
4. The first player draws and reads a clue card. If the player answers the clue correctly, he/she moves one space.
5. The player who reaches "Finish" first wins the game.

EXTENSION:
Using white bulletin board paper and crayons or tempera paint, provide time for students to work together to create a mural showing as many different forms of transportation as possible.

ASSESSMENT: Distribute the assessment worksheet and ask students to work on their own without assistance to complete them.

Vocabulary List

Transportation	Motorcycle
Transport	Canoe
Ride	Fly
Car	Travel
Train	Journey
Boat	Trip
Bus	Wagon
Bicycle	Voyage
Airplane	Traffic
Ship	Helicopter

Tracking Transportation

I ride a school bus to school everyday.

I ride on a train when

I go see my grandmother.

I lived on a boat in my country.

I came to the United States on an airplane.

Name_____ Date_____

Tracking Transportation

LEVEL THREE: ACTIVITY PAGE

Name_____ Date_____

Tracking Transportation

LEVEL FOUR ACTIVITY: TRANSPORTATION TRIVIA GAME CARDS

Go to school	Visit a next-door neighbor	Going to buy a hamburger	Rent a video
Move ahead one space	Coming to the United States	Crossing a river	Moving to a new house
Going to buy food	Take another turn	Going to the moon	Going to the mall
Bringing mail to your house	Going to the hospital	Lose one turn	Going on Vacation

Name_____ Date_____

Tracking Transportation

LEVEL FOUR: TRANSPORTATION TRIVIA BOARD GAME

Name_____ Date_____

Tracking Transportation

PORTFOLIO ASSESSMENT

Use your vocabulary words to help you write a story for your portfolio.

My Dream Trip

If I could take my dream trip, I would go to _____.

I would take _____ with me. Three means of

transportation that I would use would be _____ ,

_____ , and _____ . I would

_____

_____

_____

_____

_____

_____

_____

_____

_____

Discuss your story with your teacher. Determine with your teacher if your story shows that you understand and can use transportation words. If not, determine which words you need to work on and list them on the back of this page.

Name_____ Date_____

ESL Active Learning Lessons
Copyright ©2001 by Incentive Publications, Inc., Nashville, TN.

Understanding the Human Body

Objective:

To provide practice and reinforcement in the use of listening, speaking, reading, and writing, developing vocabulary, and acquiring basic content, concepts, and skills related to the human body.

Content Focus: SCIENCE

Materials:

- Pencils
- Paper
- Crayons
- Scissors
- Paste
- Bulletin board paper

Procedure

INTRODUCTION: Display a poster illustrating the body parts. Introduce the vocabulary words. Play the game "Simon Says" to help students learn to identify and pronounce the names of the parts of the body.

EXAMPLE: When Simon says *"touch your nose,"* Simon says *"touch your toes,"* etc., the students stand and touch the body part named. Students stay in the game until they touch the wrong body part to be "out" and must sit down. The last person standing is declared the winner of the game.

LEVEL ONE:

Instruct students to follow the directions to complete the "Clowning Around" worksheet (page 118) to help them understand the names of facial body parts.

EXTENSION:

Ask each student to draw a picture of his or her own face and label the parts.

LEVEL TWO:

Instruct students to cut out the words (page 120) and paste them on the correct body part picture (page 119).

EXTENSION:

Instruct students to cut out the body part pictures to use as flash cards. In groups of two, one student will hold up a picture and the other person will say the name of the body part.

LEVEL THREE:

Ask students to cut out the body parts (page 121) and paste them on the torso (page 122).

EXTENSION:
Students can color the complete body. Hair can be added by using ribbon or yarn. Laminate the figures and hang them as mobiles in the classroom.

LEVEL FOUR:

Distribute the "Body Parts That Go Together" worksheet (page 123). Assist students in reading aloud the words in both columns and identifying those body parts on their own bodies.

EXTENSION:
Ask students to write the words from both columns on another piece of paper, and then put the words in alphabetical order.

ASSESSMENT: Distribute the assessment worksheets (page 124). Review the procedure for working a crossword puzzle. Instruct students to use the Level Two Activity Worksheet to help with spelling the words. Instruct students to complete the assessment activity according to the directions given.

ESL Active Learning Lessons
Copyright ©2001 by Incentive Publications, Inc., Nashville, TN.

Vocabulary List

Body	Eyes
Arm	Ears
Hand	Face
Fingers	Mouth
Leg	Shoulders
Foot (Feet)	Neck
Toes	Elbow
Head	Cheeks
Hair	Ankle
Nose	Knee

ESL Active Learning Lessons
Copyright ©2001 by Incentive Publications, Inc., Nashville, TN.

Understanding the Human Body

LEVEL ONE: CLOWNING AROUND

1. Color the Clown's nose and mouth red.
2. Color the Clown's hair yellow.
3. Color the Clown's face pink.
4. Color the Clown's ears green.
5. Color the Clown's eyes brown.
6. Color the Clown's cheeks blue.

Name_____ Date_____

Understanding the Human Body

LEVEL TWO

Cut out the body part names on page 120.
Paste the correct name on each body part picture below.

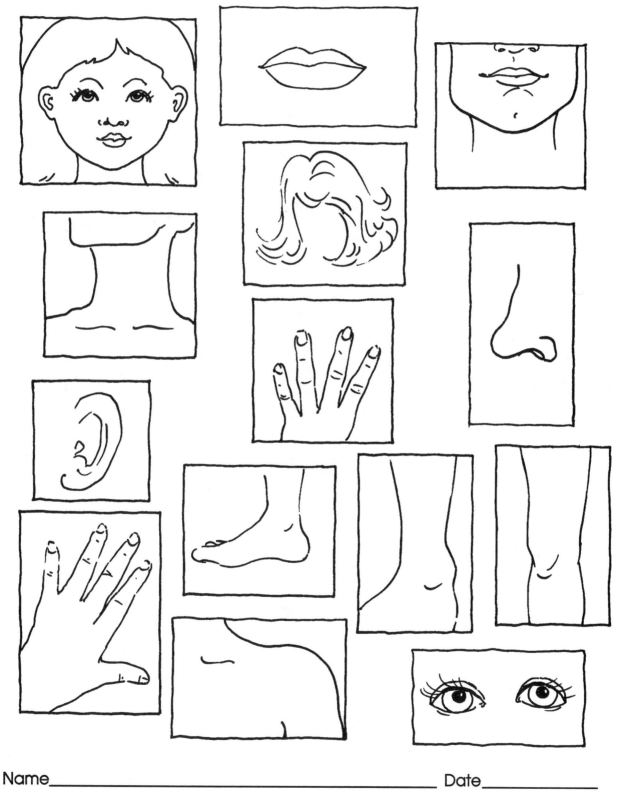

Name_____ Date_____

Understanding the Human Body

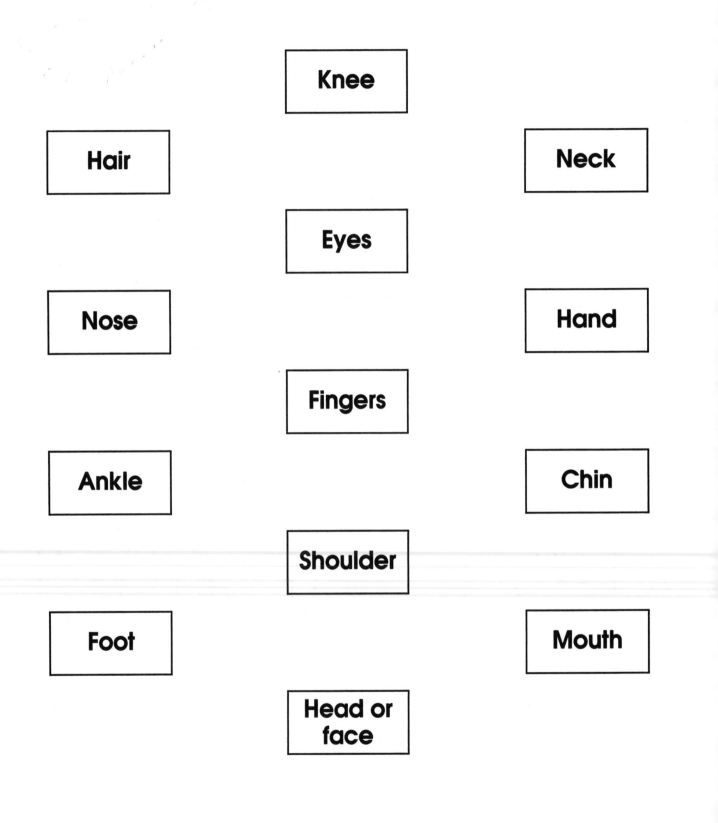

Knee

Hair

Neck

Eyes

Nose

Hand

Fingers

Ankle

Chin

Shoulder

Foot

Mouth

Head or face

Name_____ Date_____

Understanding the Human Body

LEVEL THREE

Cut out the body parts and paste them on the torso on page 122.

Name_____ Date_____

Understanding the Human Body

Cut out the torso and
paste the body
parts on it.

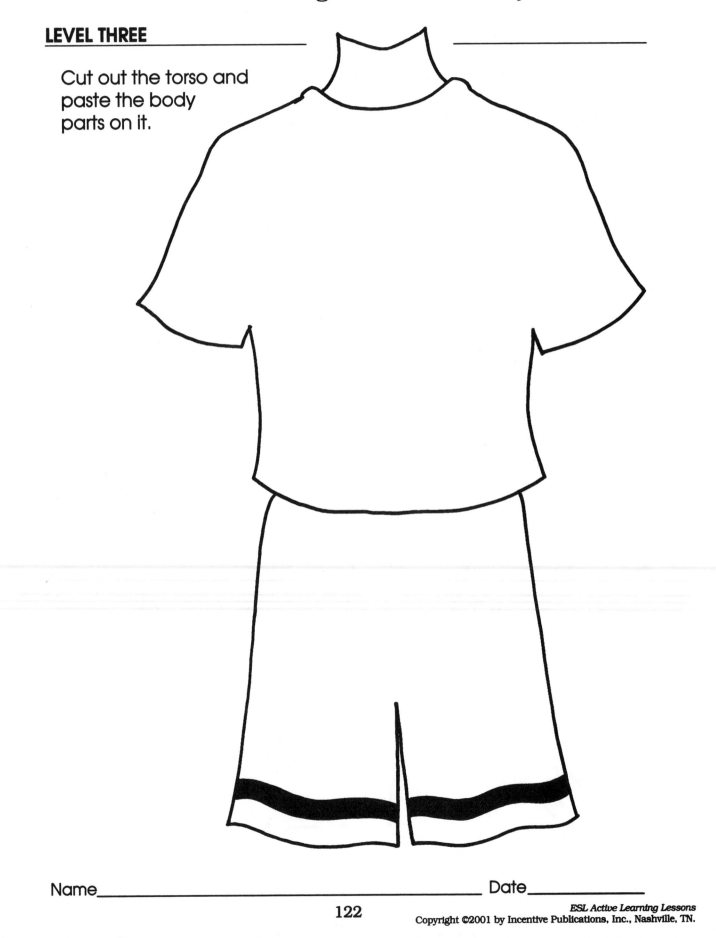

Name_____ Date_____

ESL Active Learning Lessons
Copyright ©2001 by Incentive Publications, Inc., Nashville, TN.

Understanding the Human Body

LEVEL FOUR: BODY PARTS THAT GO TOGETHER

Draw a line to match each body part in column one with the part it belongs with in column two. The first one has been done for you as an example.

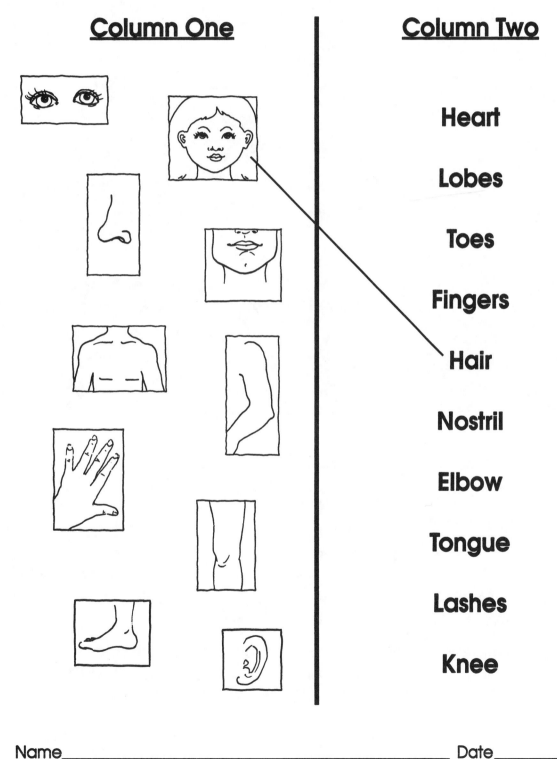

Column One

Column Two

Heart

Lobes

Toes

Fingers

Hair

Nostril

Elbow

Tongue

Lashes

Knee

Name_____ Date_____

Understanding the Human Body

ASSESSMENT: BODY BUSINESS

DOWN

2. This body part is on a foot.
5. This body part is on each side of the neck.
6. This is used for eating.
7. There are ten of these on a pair of hands.
9. This body part is connected to the foot.
10. This body part has eyes, nose, and mouth on it.
11. You smell with this body part.
12. This body part is in the middle of the leg.

ACROSS

1. Fingers are on this body part.
3. This body part is between the shoulders and the hand.
4. This body part is used to see.
8. You can comb and brush this body part.
10. These are attached to the bottom of legs.
11. This connects a face and a body.
13. This is the number of fingers and toes there are.
14. You hear with these.
15. This body part is in the middle of an arm.

Give yourself a score of two points for each correctly-answered item on the crossword puzzle.

Arrange a conference to discuss your score and to correctly pronounce and identify each body part named in the puzzle. Write a journal entry summarizing your understanding of your own body and the purpose of various parts.

Name_____ Date_____

Using Important Information

Objective:

To provide practice in using the English language, extending vocabulary, using critical thinking skills, and developing an awareness of important information for use in everyday situations.

Content Focus: LIFE SKILLS

Materials:

- Pencils
- Paper
- Telephone directories
- Bulletin board paper
- Boxes
- Crayons or colored pencils

Procedure:

LEVEL ONE:

1. Ask each student to bring a box from home. Cereal, shoe, detergent, and candy boxes work well. Have a few boxes on hand for those students who may forget or do not have access to a box from home (or use page 128).
2. Provide art materials for students to cover the boxes to create their homes. If students live in an apartment, two boxes can be stacked together. Tempera paint or markers can be used to add detail to the houses.
3. Instruct students to write his or her address on the houses. Emphasize the importance of using capital letters, correct spelling, and appropriate punctuation.
4. Display the houses to stimulate conversation and discussion.

EXTENSION:

Place a long piece of bulletin board paper on the floor. Using art supplies, draw a neighborhood map. Label and color the streets, sidewalks, trees, etc. Arrange the houses and apartments that were made for the Level One activity on the map.

LEVEL TWO:

Ask students to listen to the home safety rules as they are read aloud. Then think of other home safety rules. Write these rules in the blank window of the house on page 129. Have students read the safety rules with a partner.

EXTENSION:

Direct students to make a list of rules that will help their family be safe at home, then draw a picture that shows how safety was practiced in the homes of their native country.

LEVEL THREE:

1. Divide the class into groups of three.
2. Provide a telephone directory for each group and lead a class discussion on how to use it.

3. Distribute the worksheets (page 130) and ask each group to use the telephone directory to complete the exercise.

EXTENSION:

Direct students to work in groups of two. Using the Business Section of the telephone directory, find the following telephone numbers, then write the name of the business and the telephone number for the following places.

Place to buy pizza _____

A movie theatre _____

A restaurant _____

A video rental store _____

A post office _____

Place to buy hamburgers _____

A toy store _____

A gas station _____

A drug store _____

A bank _____

Find 4 other business numbers: _____

_____

LEVEL FOUR:

1. School records must carry certain important information to be used in the event of an emergency during the school day. Lead a class discussion about the importance of this information as it relates to pupil safety and security. Tell the students that all school records are strictly confidential.
2. Ask each student to complete the "Personal Information File" (page 131) with up-to-date information.

EXTENSION:

Using the cards that were filled out in the Level Four activity, instruct students to work together in groups of two (one student is the student, the other is the parent) to pretend to telephone a parent to report or request the following:

1. The student is sick, and the parent needs to come and get him or her.
2. An important signed paper was left at home.
3. Permission is requested to invite a friend to your home after school.
4. School is dismissed early because of snow or a bad storm.
5. The student forgot lunch money.

Assessment:

Distribute the assessment worksheets. Instruct students to complete the assessment activity according to the directions given.

126

Vocabulary List

Important	Directory
Information	Long distance
Telephone	Contact
Phone number	Strictly
Record	Confidential
Address	Area code
Ride	Strangers
Walk	Dial
Emergency	Acquire
Telephone	Personal

Using Important Information

LEVEL ONE

Name_____ Date_____

Using Important Information

Call 911 for help.

Other safety rules:

Other safety rules:

Be sure the water is not too hot.

Turn off the stove after use.

Keep the doors locked.

Do not let strangers in the house.

Other safety rules:

Name_____ Date_____

Using Important Information

LEVEL THREE: USING THE TELEPHONE DIRECTORY

Complete the following exercise.

1. What is the area code for your city? _____

2. What is the emergency number
   for the police? _____

3. How can you get an operator? _____

4. If you don't know a telephone
   number, what number do you dial? _____

5. How do you make a long distance
   call in the United States? _____

6. List the telephone number for each person in your group.

   _____   _____

   _____   _____

   _____   _____

   _____   _____

   _____   _____

   _____   _____

7. List the telephone number for a
   grocery store in your neighborhood. _____

8. List the name and telephone number
   of the first person in the directory. _____

9. List the name and telephone number
   of the last person in the directory. _____

10. What is the telephone number
    of your school? _____

Name_____ Date_____

130

Using Important Information

Personal Information

Name: _____ _____ _____
        (Last)   (First)   (Middle)

Age: _____ Grade: _____

Classroom teacher: _____

Home telephone: _____

Address: _____ (House or
                                    Apartment Number)
         _____ (street)
         _____ (City)
         _____ (state)
         _____ (Zip)

Parent(s) or Guardian: _____

Business telephone: _____

Person to contact if unable to reach
    parent or guardian:

    Name: _____
    Telephone: _____

Name_____ Date_____

Using Important Information Check-Up

1. (√) Can recognize word
   (√+) Can recognize and pronounce word
   (√++) Can recognize, pronounce, and tell the meaning of word

Vocabulary Words:

_____ Important		_____ Directory
_____ Information		_____ Long distance
_____ Telephone		_____ Contact
_____ Phone number		_____ Strictly
_____ Record		_____ Confidential
_____ Address		_____ Area code
_____ Ride		_____ Strangers
_____ Walk		_____ Dial
_____ Emergency		_____ Acquire
_____ Telephone		_____ Personal

2. Three home safety rules that I remember are:

   1. _____

   2. _____

   3. _____

3. My Understanding of the use of the telephone directory is:

   Fine   O.K.   Not so good

Name_____ Date_____

Watching the Weather

Objective:
To provide reinforcement and practice in the use of listening, speaking, reading and writing skills, and in the acquisition of content concepts related to weather.

Content Focus: SCIENCE

Materials:
- Thermometer
- Measuring cup
- Pencils
- Paper

Procedure:
INTRODUCTION: Verbally introduce the "Watching the Weather" unit. Display pictures of different weather scenes if possible and provide time for discussion of causes, effects, and importance of weather. Present the twenty vocabulary words and discuss each one. Pass out vocabulary worksheets to be used for reference and reinforcement.

LEVEL ONE:

1. Explain the following terms as causes and effects of weather: temperature, air pressure, wind, and moisture.
2. Explain how a thermometer measures temperature. Degrees are used to read a thermometer. Demonstrate how degrees are written.
3. Discuss how the Fahrenheit scale is used to read temperature in the United States, while in other countries, the centigrade scale is used. Ask students to contribute to a discussion of how temperature is read in their native countries.
4. Supply a thermometer for students to examine and become familiar with.
5. Complete the worksheet on page 136 according to directions.

EXTENSION:
Keep a class weather log for one week by measuring and recording the temperature on the weather log each day.

LEVEL TWO:

1. Discuss the four types of clouds.
   Cirrus: Thin wispy clouds high in the sky.
   Stratus: Thick layers of clouds low in the sky.
   Cumulus: Big puffy or piles of clouds that start low and rise high in the sky.
   Cumulonimbus: Large, gray thunderclouds.
2. Take the class outside to observe the clouds.
3. Distribute the worksheets on page 137 and instruct students to complete the Maze Activity by "flying" the plane from their native country to the United States. As a cloud is passed, identify its type by writing the name on the line.

EXTENSION:
Remind students that sometimes clouds look like shapes of animals, people, or objects. Provide time and supplies for them to work as partners to draw cumulus clouds in different shapes. Display completed works for other partner groups to identify and discuss the shapes.

LEVEL THREE:

1. Explain the weather cycle as follows: *Tiny drops of water are in the clouds. When the water becomes too heavy inside a cloud, it rains.* Provide time for students to understand this fact about rain. *Sometimes a rainbow occurs during or after a rain. The sun shining through droplets of water causes rainbows. The colors of a rainbow are red, orange, yellow, green, blue, indigo, and violet. The colors are always in the same order.* Ask students to share experiences of where, when, and under what circumstances they have seen rainbows.
2. Complete the rainbow (page 138) with the colors in the correct order.

EXTENSION:
1. Use a measuring cup or a rain gauge to measure the rainfall. Place the measuring cup outside to collect the rain. Keep a record of the rainfall and compare the amounts for several weeks.
2. Draw the water cycle.

LEVEL FOUR:

1. Discuss thunderstorms, blizzards, tornadoes, and hurricanes.
2. Take the students to the library to find resource books to use to gain a complete understanding of the different kinds of storms.
3. Distribute worksheets and provide colored pencils for students to use to illustrate the various kinds of storms (page 139).

EXTENSION:
1. Divide the class into groups of two. Ask each group to prepare a weather report. Let students pretend to be on television and give the weather reports.
2. If possible, take a field trip to a television station to see how weather is reported. If it is not possible, invite a weather reporter to visit the classroom.

Assessment
Distribute the performance check-up word find puzzle and discuss directions and scoring key. Allow time for completion and follow-up conferences with students.

Vocabulary List

Temperature	Cirrus
Air pressure	Stratus
Wind	Cumulus
Moisture	Cumulonimbus
Degree	Evaporation
Sunny	Rainbow
Rain	Thunderstorm
Water cycle	Blizzard
Snow	Tornado
Clouds	Hurricane

Watching the Weather

LEVEL ONE WORKSHEET

DIRECTIONS: Read each thermometer. Under each thermometer, draw a picture of yourself dressed in clothes that would be appropriate for the temperature. Remember that the thermometers go up and down by two-degree steps.

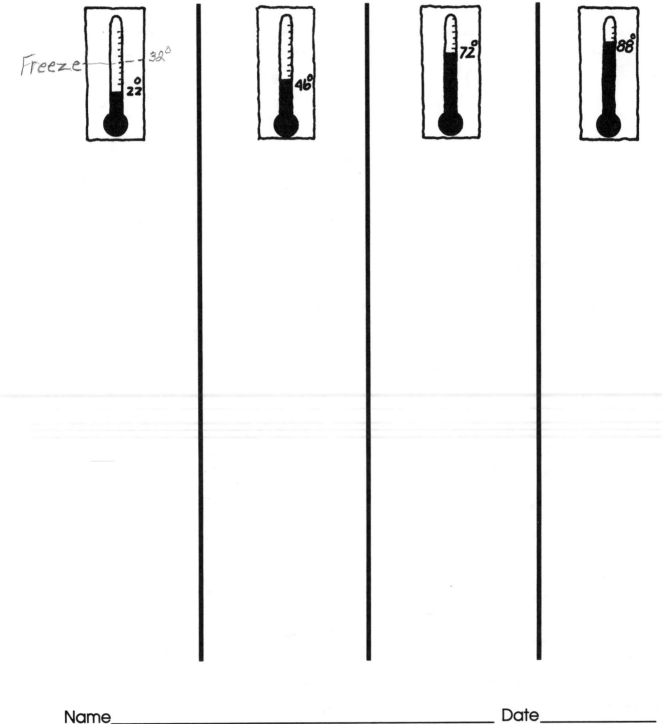

Watching the Weather

LEVEL TWO

I am from _____

Name_____ Date_____

Watching the Weather

LEVEL THREE: RAINBOW ACTIVITY

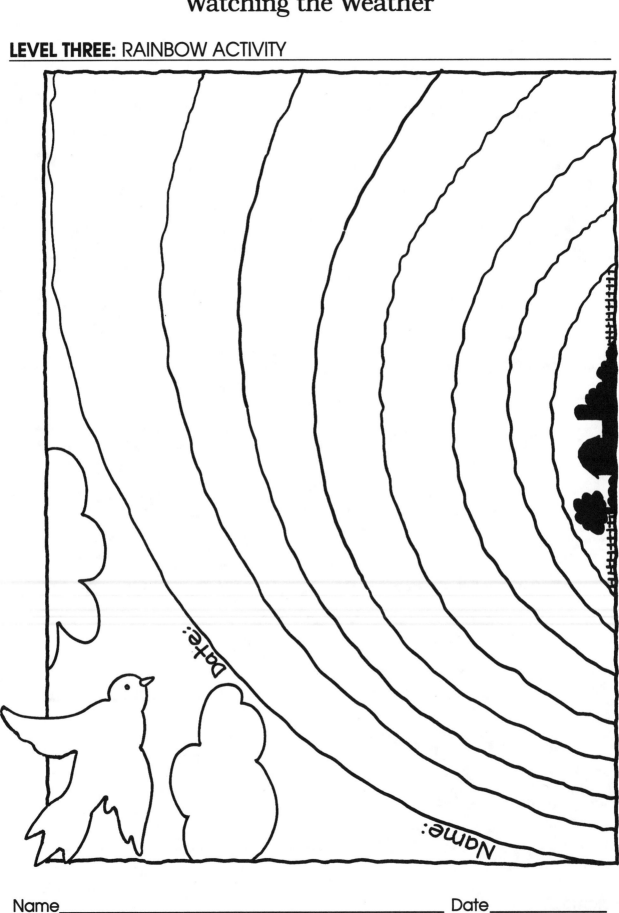

Name_____ Date_____

Watching the Weather

LEVEL FOUR: STORMS

Thunderstorm	Blizzard
Tornado	Hurricane

Name_____ Date_____

Watching the Weather Check-up

PERFORMANCE ASSESSMENT

Find each of the words from the word list in the word search puzzle. Words may go up, down, and across, but never backwards or diagonally. Words to find:

Thunderstorm
Rain
Snow
Thunder
Lightning
Temperature
Degrees
Tornado
Hurricane
Weather
Sunny
Fog
Wind
Water cycle
Cumulus
Stratus
Cumulonimbus
Rainbow
Evaporation
Cloud
Sun
Weather

```
B Q T E M P E R A T U R E T
E R A I N C B L R N O P W U
D A S Q C M C L O U D F A Q
T I W E A T H E R S A R T E
F N O G S H U D N T N J E M
E B N T E U G O U V R H R R
V O S H W N I U F A O P C O
A W V G J D Q I X K T B Y T
P J Y F D E G R E E S K C S
O X H O L R C Z K R H C L R
R L I G H T N I N G L U E E
A M S Y W I N D A M I M P D
T N H U R R I C A N E U B N
I S U N N Y O N Z J C L Q U
O C U M U L O N I M B U S H
N P D O A S T R A T U S K T
```

SCORING KEY:

20 to 22 words: 20 points   19 to 12 words: 10 points   11 or less words: 5 points
For every word you can pronounce, give yourself 2 points. For every word you can give the meaning of, give yourself 4 additional points.

My score _____

Name_____ Date_____

Annotated Bibliography
for the ESL Teacher

COOPERATIVE LEARNING TEACHER TIMESAVERS. Imogene Forte. Nashville, Incentive Publications, Inc., 1992
> Contains summaries, warm-ups, bulletin boards, cooperative activities, and motivational ideas, as well as ready-to-use reproducible aids, badges, clip art, reports, worksheets, and records.

CREATING CONNECTIONS: Learning to Appreciate Diversity. Dorothy Michener. Nashville, Incentive Publications Inc., 1995
> Provides practical strategies and workable solutions for educators striving to help their students recognize, understand, and appreciate diversity.

EASY ART PROJECTS TO TEACH GLOBAL AWARENESS. Lynn Brisson. Nashville, Incentive Publications Inc., 1993
> Topics covered include map skills, the 50 United States, the 7 continents, desert and ocean study, and more!

HANDS-ON MATH. Kathleen Fletcher. Nashville, Incentive Publications Inc., 1996
> Contains all the essentials and extras for teaching number-sense concepts. Included ideas for using stamps, stickers, beans, rice, tiles, and number lines in the classroom.

KIDS' STUFF BOOK OF READING AND LANGUAGE ARTS, PRIMARY. Imogene Forte and Joy MacKenzie. Nashville, Incentive Publications Inc., 1989
> Provides teacher-directed lessons and reproducible, high-interest activities for every area of the primary language arts curriculum: speaking and listening, word recognition and usage, comprehension and reading independence, grammar and spelling, writing, independence, and study skills.

KIDS STUFF MATH, PRIMARY. Marge Frank. Nashville, Incentive Publications Inc., 1988
> Provides teacher-directed lessons and reproducible, high-interest activities for every area of the primary math curriculum: number concepts, addition and subtraction, multiplication and division, fractions and decimals, time and money, measurement, geometry, graphing, and problem solving.

LANGUAGE ARTS FOLDER FUN. Kathy Blankenhorn and Joanne Richards. Nashville, Incentive Publications Inc., 1995
> Folder games target and reinforce the fundamentals of language arts.

LEARNING GAMES WITHOUT LOSERS. Sarah Liu and Mary Lou Vittitow. Nashville, Incentive Publications Inc., 1985
> These non-competitive learning games were designed to meet the needs of students with different backgrounds and abilities.

LEARNING TO LEARN: Strengthening Study Skills and Brain Power. Gloria Frender. Nashville, Incentive Publications Inc., 1990
> Includes step-by-step procedures for improving organizational skills, time management, problem solving, power reading, test taking, memory skills, and more!

MULTICULTURAL PLAYS: A Many-Splendored Tapestry Honoring Our Global Community. Judy Mecca. Nashville, Incentive Publications Inc., 1999
> Easily-produced plays allow students to learn about and develop respect for different cultures. A brief cultural lesson accompanies each play to ensure an authentic performance.

READ ABOUT IT, PRIMARY READERS. Imogene Forte. Nashville, Incentive Publications Inc., 1982
> Focuses on word recognition, word usage, and independent reading skills.

READING REINFORCERS FOR THE PRIMARY GRADES. Imogene Forts. Nashville, Incentive Publications Inc., 1994
> A collection of teacher-directed interactive projects, creative worksheets, and independent and group activities.

SELLING SPELLING TO KIDS. Imogene Forte and Mary Ann Pangle. Nashville, Incentive Publications Inc., 1985
> By providing lists of spelling rules, problem words, and more, this practical resource will help students become first-rate spellers.

SOMETHING SPECIAL: Basic Skills Activity Units for Primary Grade Kids Who Need Extra Help in Reading. Cherrie Farnette, Imogene Forte, and Barbara Loss. Nashville, Incentive Publications Inc., 1982
> Provides student assessment, followed by skills-based units coded to three levels of difficulty. Units cover comprehension, word identification and usage.

THINK ABOUT IT, PRIMARY. Imogene Forte. Nashville, Incentive Publications Inc., 1981.
> Contains reproducible activities that deal with listening, questioning, brainstorming, interpreting, predicting, estimating, and more.

USING LITERATURE TO LEARN ABOUT CHILDREN AROUND THE WORLD. Judith Cochran. Nashville, Incentive Publications Inc., 1993
> Lesson plans outline specific activities to develop social and global awareness and to strengthen vocabulary and thinking skills.

WRITE ABOUT IT, PRIMARY. Imogene Forte. Nashville, Incentive Publications Inc., 1983
> Covers skills related to vocabulary development, technical writing, composition, and original writing.

Answer Page

Page 14

These words should be circled in the word search:
Right, Left, In, Out, On, Under, Up, Down, Beside, Between, Forward, Backward, Across, Around, Ahead, Behind, North, South, East, West

Page 16

1. Check to be sure students have named the continents correctly.
2–3. Answers will vary.
4. West; South; North; North-West; North; East; East; South; West
5. Answers will vary

Page 24

Fruits that grow on trees are: apples, oranges, cherries, limes, bananas, and pears.
Fruits that grow on vines are: strawberries, cantaloupe, grapes, and watermelon.
More fruits grow on trees than on vines.

Page 25

1. $0.40; $3.60
2. two; $4.50; three
3. $0.30; $0.18
4. Answers will vary; Answers will vary; 300
5. 30 cans

Page 30

Spoon, Chair, Fork, Napkin, Tray, Knife, Table, Cashier

Page 58

1. $1.35
2. Answers will vary; one possible answer: 1 dollar, 1 quarter, and 1 dime
3. $.65
4. Answers will vary; one possible answer: 1 half dollar, 1 dime, and 1 nickel
5. Circle popsicle
6. $6.75
7. Answers will vary; one possible answer: 1 five-dollar bill, 1 dollar bill, and 3 quarters
8. $0.25
9. Answers will vary; one possible answer: quarter
10. Circle 3 quarters and 2 dimes
    or
    3 quarters, 1 dime, and 2 nickels

Page 65

1. 2
2. 6
3. 1
4. $\frac{1}{2}$
5. 3
6. 1; 6
7. 9
8. 1; 12
9. 2; 3
10. 15
11. 4
12. 1; 8

Page 66

10 pounds of meat;
5 bun packages;
6 dozen cans;
4 pounds of potatoes;
3 pounds of rice;
1 dozen cans of beans;
25 pounds of chicken;
10 dozen cookies;
48 ounces of ice cream;
80 ounces

Page 67

1. $1.77; 48 ounces
2. 1 half-gallon / or 8 cups
3. $6.95
4. 16 cups
5. 10-pound bag is cheaper by $1.50
6. Six; $1.20
7. 1 pound, 8 ounces
8. 16; 1 pound; 2 pounds

Page 118

Be sure student drawing of clown face matches instructions.

Page 119

Check to be sure each body part is in the correct word box.

Page 124

Down
2. Ankle
5. Shoulder
6. Mouth
7. Fingers
9. Leg
10. Face
11. Nose
12. Knee

Across
1. Hand
3. Arm
4. Eyes
8. Hair
10. Feet
11. Neck
13. Ten
14. Ears
15. Elbow

Pages 130–131

Answers will vary.